New Hall

New Hall

THE HISTORY OF ENGLAND IN ONE HOUSE

Written by Kate Holt
with Charlotte Eagar

Foreword by A. David Owen OBE; MA (Cantab)

CLEARVIEWBOOKS

First published in the UK in 2022 by

CLEARVIEWBOOKS

99 Priory Park Road
London NW6 7UX
www.clearviewbooks.com

ISBN 978-1908337-627

Editor: **Catharine Snow**
Editorial & Research: **Kate Holt** and **Charlotte Eagar**
Design: **Lucy Gowans**
Production: **Rosanna Dickinson**

A CIP record of this book is available from the British Library.

Printed in Croatia.

Contents

Foreword by A. David Owen OBE; MA (Cantab)

It is time to tell the story of New Hall in a magnificently illustrated book by Kate Holt. This project has developed as result of my long friendship with Kate's father, Dr Bev Holt with whom I shared rooms at university. Subsequently he and his wife invited me to be Kate's godfather.

Kate's career as a photographer has included a significant number of photographic exhibitions both in London and elsewhere, including a recent one at the Midland Arts Centre in Birmingham entitled 'Brave Girls of South Sudan.' For this present book, Kate has researched the Birmingham Library for some of the older photographs and has also taken original photographs herself.

Part One of the book in its first nine chapters tells the story of each owner and the families who lived there, leading to its ownership today as a remarkable hotel. This has ensured that the people of Sutton Coldfield and elsewhere can enjoy the Hall's magnificent medieval and Tudor interiors and beautifully landscaped gardens, whether for lunch, a short stay, a conference or a wedding.

Part Two of the book covers the development of the New Hall estate with its three distinct farms, and New Hall Water Mill which ground their corn into flour. The Mill, which is a pleasant stroll from the hotel, is working again today and run by the Friends of New Hall Mill who are all volunteers. The Mill is greatly valued by the community who visit on Open Days with nearly a thousand visitors on a fine Bank Holiday.

I hope this book will be enjoyed by many with the story that it tells and the superb photographs, some hitherto unseen, that it contains

AD OWEN
September 2022

LEFT: A benign and regulatory-free visit to New Hall's roof by the Sutton Coldfield Preservation Society in the 1950's. The opening of the new railway line in 1879, and the frenzied building developments that accompanied it, prompted local groups to ensure the preservation of as much natural parkland as possible. New Hall and Sutton Coldfield were in the eye of a suburban tsunami.

Introduction

New Hall glows with local sandstone and warm Midlands brick. It sits in its valley, embraced by thick woods, just outside the age-old town of Sutton Coldfield, in what was for hundreds of years the ancient County of Warwick. One of the oldest inhabited moated houses in England, New Hall once sat in the vast hunting forests of Sutton Chase, but now the spreading mass of Birmingham is at the gates - kept at bay by the green spaces of New Hall Country Park. Sir Nicholas Pevsner, the great 20th century British architectural historian, describes New Hall in his guide to the houses of Warwickshire, as a "major mansion in a moat, but a puzzling one." He writes of the plaster ceilings, the Solar (known as the Great Chamber), the seventeenth century staircase and various other editions to the medieval house – Elizabethan, Georgian and High Victorian – which seem so in tune, sometimes it's hard to see where one addition ends and the other begins. But when New Hall's first stones were laid, over 800 years ago, its four-square crenellations were built for defence, not decoration. The house was added to and adorned by subsequent owners, whose fortunes rose and fell in the cycle of their times. It is a house that has lasted almost a millennium and the light bouncing off the lily-filled moat, its diamond-shard mullioned windows, their rippling ancient glass, the elegant hubris of the Victorian cupola-ed, castellated wing, all mirror England's story.

New Hall has witnessed momentous events. New Hall's address now is the modern County of the West Midlands, and as such, is built on a region that straddles the nation's heart and was of enormous strategic importance for centuries. New Hall has been owned or visited by some of the most influential people in English history. Henry VIII is said to have stayed at the hall and hunted nearby in the game-filled Royal forests of Sutton Chase, since New Hall then belonged to the family of his friend and counsellor Bishop Vesey. Before the Tudors emerged victorious from England's 15th century civil wars, New Hall had been a hunting lodge of the Earls of Warwick for generations; it had belonged to Warwick the Kingmaker, the great dynamo of the Wars of the Roses. As the power of the Great Magnates, like Warwick, died under the Tudors, and the landed gentry rose, the Hall spent four hundred years owned by successive Knights of the Shires: the Gibbons who got rich during the Reformation; the Sacheverells, a family of ancient of Norman gentry, who held out for Charles I, and allegedly hid Charles II when he was on the run, during the Civil War; the Chadwicks, who played their part in Victoria's empire in India but went bust during the late 19th century Great Agricultural Depression. After a blip as a boys' school in the late 19th century – for the depression had destroyed many land-owners' fortunes – New Hall and its estates then passed into the hands of the Wilkinsons, commercial giants from nearby Birmingham. In the early 1900's, New Hall was bought by the great 20th century engineering dynasty of Alfred Ernest Owen, who made his money through early innovations in the world of motor cars.

New Hall, like so many ancient houses, has now been turned into a hotel: its Great Chamber and Yew Walk are now frequented by the modern aristocracies of Rock, Opera and acting, such as Kylie Minogue and Luciano Pavarotti; brides wanting the glamour of medieval romance hire New Hall for their weddings, people come and stay who just want peace and quiet in magical surroundings. New Hall once stood surrounded by its own estates, rich farms, densely forested woods - much of which is now built over or part of Sutton Country Park, where the folk of Sutton Coldfield wander with their dogs or bicycle. But the ghosts of New Hall's ancient past still walk, side by side with the rock stars, brides and staff, the walkers and the cyclists.

The fortunes and history of New Hall can be traced through the six main properties that still stand: the ancient house itself, still sitting inside its moat and forested demesne, Wincelle, New Shipton Farm, Warren House, Ford Keepers Cottage and New Hall Mill – all of which formed part of the New Hall Estate. And the history of this house, its farms and land, in its way, is a microcosm of the history of England itself.

New Hall Timeline

Pre 1066
Saxon Earls of Mercia

1066
Norman Conquest

1126
Henry 1st gave Manor of Sutton Coldfield to the Earl of Warwick

1200 (circa)
A Hall one mile south of Sutton Coldfield first built

1340
Enlarged and rebuilt and called New Hall

Owned by Sir John Lizours
First known written confirmation

1425
New Shipton Farm barns built

1520
New Hall recorded as owned by William Gibbons. Gibbons' brother-in-law, Bishop John Vesey, starts to construct 51 houses around Sutton Coldfield, including Ford Keeper's Cottage

1552
Hall recorded to be owned by Thomas Gibbons of Ditchley, William's son

1575
Thomas Gibbons dies. His eldest son, Thomas, inherits the Hall but doesn't want to live there
First mention of two mill cottages as part of estate documents

1586
Thomas rents out New Hall to Percy Willoughby of Nottingham

1589
Rent expires and Thomas sells New Hall to his brother William Gibbons

1592
William Gibbons dies and his wife Mary continues living at New Hall

1595
First record of Warren Farmhouse

1608
Mary Gibbons dies leaving four sons

1610
Hall sold by Gibbons family to Henry Sacheverell of Ratby, Co. Leics for £1880

1613
Sacheverell transfers ownership of New Hall to his 9 year old son - Valens

1628
Last member of Gibbons family – Ursula – dies – it is thought she was still living in the Hall

1629
Valens Sacheverell moves into New Hall

1660
Valens dies after living in the Hall for many years, and leaves it to his son - George

1715
George Sacheverell dies and leaves the Hall to a nephew by marriage – Charles Chadwick

1750
New Shipton Farmhouse built

1779
Charles Chadwick dies leaving New Hall to his unmarried sister Dorothy

1784
Dorothy Chadwick dies leaving New Hall to her uncle, Ralph Foyer of Hints

1824
Enclosures Act passed

1829
Charles Chadwick III dies and New Hall is passed to Hugo Malveysin Chadwick

1854
Hugo Malveysin Chadwick dies leaving New Hall to John de Healey Chadwick

1861
John de Healey Chadwick leases the Mill for 21 years to Dutton brothers of Sutton Coldfield

1870
North wing and bridge over the moat are added

1882
John de Healey Chadwick goes bankrupt and has to sell New Hall

1885
New Hall opens as a school for boys

1903
New Hall sold to Lt Col Wilkinson who restores it to a family home

1910
Wincelle House moved to its current location

1923
Alfred Ernest Owen purchases New Hall

1929
Alfred Ernest Owen dies – his wife Florence Lucy Beech Owen stays on living in New Hall

1958
Florence Owen dies

1962
Sir Alfred George Beech Owen moves into New Hall with his family

1975
Sir Alfred George Beech Owen dies and New Hall is vacated

1985
New Hall sold to Thistle hotel group
New Hall Mill opened to the public

1990
New Hall Valley Country Park opened

1992
New Wing Built

1997
Sutton Country Park designated National Nature Reserve and listed by English Heritage

2008
Hand Picked Hotels group buy New Hall

2020
Covid Pandemic Hits – Sutton and New Hall Country Park's green spaces become more important than ever

PART ONE

THE HOUSE

1.

THE DARK AGES AND BEYOND: THE EARLS OF MERCIA, SUTTON COLDFIELD AND THE NORMAN CONQUEST

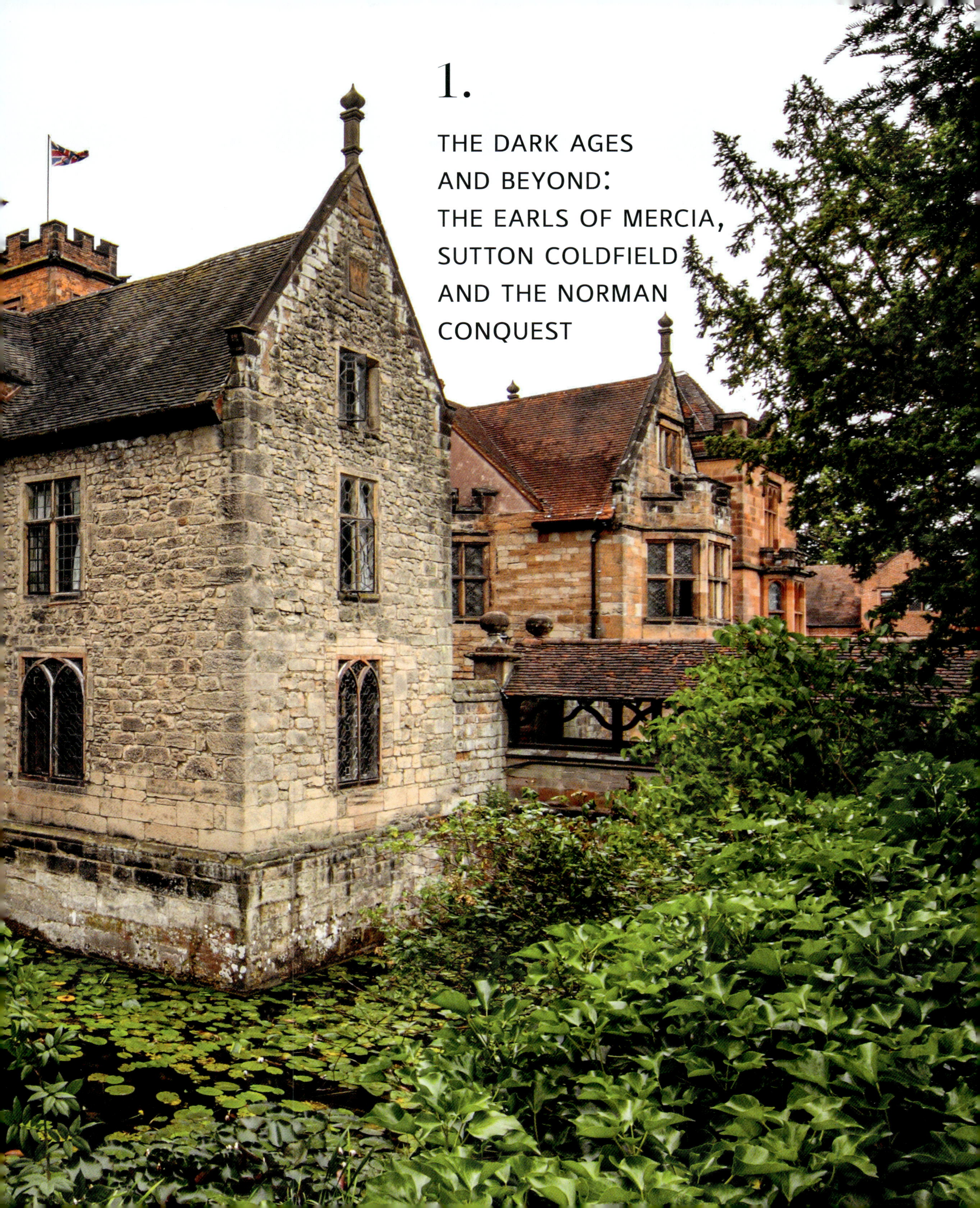

ANGLO-SAXON BRITAIN
"THE HEPTARCHY."
English Miles
0 10 20 40 60 80
PICTS
Forth
Alcluyd
STRATHCLYDE
GALLOWAY
Lindisfarne
Tweed
BERNICIA
NORTHUMBRIA
Tyne
Jarrow
Durham
Tees
Whitby
Man
Degsastan ×603
Swale
DEIRA
York
Wharfe
Heathfield ×633
Humber
Manchester
LINDSEY
Dore
Trent
Lincoln
Chester ×607 & 613
Faddiley ×584
Nottingham
Derby
Maserfield ×642
Stafford
MIDDLE ANGLES
Leicester
Tamworth
Lichfield
NORTH GYRWE
Stamford
NORTH WALES
Severn
MERCIA
(MIERCE)
SOUTH GYRWE
EAST ANGLES
Bridgenorth
Warwick
Fen
Ouse
St. Edmundsbury
HWICCE
SOUTH ANGLES
Gloucester
Burford
Witham
Hertford
EAST SAXONS
Oxford ×774
Bensington ×777
MIDDLE SAXONS
London
Thames
Ashdown ×871
Deorham ×577
Englefield ×871
Reading ×871
Chippenham
Merton ×871
Wedmore
WESSEX
Ethandun ×878
Ockley ×851
KENT
Ellandun ×825
Winchester
Athelney
Wilton ×871
Sherborne
SOUTH SAXONS
Wareham
Wight
Hengests Dun ×836
WEST WALES
FRISIA

THE DARK AGES AND BEYOND: THE EARLS OF MERCIA, SUTTON COLDFIELD AND THE NORMAN CONQUEST

OPPOSITE: The Heptarchy is the collective name applied to the seven petty Kingdoms of Anglo-Saxon England, from the Anglo-Saxon settlement of Britain in the 5th century until the 8th century consolidation into the four kingdoms of Mercia, Northumbria, Wessex and East Anglia. New Hall is marked by a red dot in the centre of Mercia.

Before the Norman Conquest of 1066, the manor of Sutton Coldfield and the lands around it - on which New Hall was later built - were part of the vast estates owned by Edwin, Earl of Mercia. Mercia had been an independent Kingdom between 527-879 AD, a powerful Anglo-Saxon political entity located in the midlands of present-day England, with its capital at nearby Tamworth. Mercia was bordered by rival Kingdoms - Wessex on the south, Wales to the west, on the north by Northumbria, and on the east, by East Anglia. The rulers of Mercia allegedly had a hunting lodge near Sutton, amongst the richly wooded ranges of Sutton Chase. By the tenth century, Mercia had long been incorporated into the Anglo-Saxon Kingdom of England, and Mercia was one of the great Earldoms of the country and, a hundred years later, just before the Norman Conquest, Earl Edwin of Mercia and his family were at the heart of Anglo-Saxon aristocratic and royal power. Earl Edwin's sister, Lady Ealdgyth, was married to King Harold Godwinson, himself.

990–1067
Lady Godiva

Earl Edwin and Lady Eadlgyth were the grandchildren of the notorious Lady Godiva, Countess of Mercia, who is said to have ridden ridden naked through the streets of nearby Coventry. Lady Godiva, the story goes, had been long begging her husband, Earl Leofric of Mercia, to lift what she felt were unfair tax burdens on the local populace. The exasperated Earl apparently agreed, on the condition that his wife – who was famously beautiful - stripped and rode nude through the town. Much to the Earl's probable surprise and chagrin, strip Lady Godiva did. After issuing a proclamation that the people of Coventry should stay indoors, their shutters closed, so no-one could see her, Lady Godiva set off on horseback, clothed only in her long hair. Her orders were obeyed by everyone except a tailor, who could not resist sneaking a look at this naked aristocratic beauty: as a result, he has gone down in history as Peeping Tom. Earl Leofric, however, did allegedly honour his promise and cancel the taxes. As there are no surviving written records of this story until the 13th century, some 200 years after the event, it is possible that the story may be untrue but, true or not, Lady Godiva's nude heroism has inspired numerous artists over the centuries.

OPPOSITE: These menacing dragons stand at the main entrance to New Hall and form part of the crest of the Gibbons family, owners during the 1500's.

FOLLOWING PAGES: The ability to put a moat around your house for defence purposes in the Middle Ages was paramount, and New Hall was surrounded by up to seven freshwater springs. A drawbridge was then erected, later turned into a permanent walkway after the Wars of the Roses ended.

1066
King Harold, Queen Ealdgyth and William the Conqueror

Lady Godiva lived to see the downfall of her family. In 1066, the manor of Sutton Coldfield was owned by the powerful Earls of Mercia. Lady Godiva's grand-daughter, Lady Ealdgyth, Earl Edwin of Mercia's sister, was Queen of England, married to King Harold Godwinson. A great beauty, she had previously been married to the Welsh King Gryffuth ap Llewellyn. King Gryffuth was killed in 1063, when King Harold Godwinson invaded Wales; Queen Ealdgyth then married King Harold instead. This was a marriage designed to strengthen the ties between the powerful Earls of Mercia and the Crown. However, in the autumn of 1066, England was attacked by a two-pronged invasion – King Harald Hardrada of Norway landed in the North in September. Earl Edwin and his brother Morcar, Earl of Northumberland, tried to fight off Hardrada at York on 20th September, but lost. King Harold Godwinson, as a result, had to come north; he defeated and killed Hardrada at the Battle of Stamford Bridge. But to King Harold Godwinson's horror, three weeks later, on 14th October, William the Conqueror invaded Kent. King Harold Godwinson hastened south, only to be felled by an arrow in the eye and Queen Ealdgyth was widowed for the second time in three years.

1068
The Saxon Pushback

In 1068, Edwin and Morcar, Earl of Northumberland, raised a rebellion in Mercia against the Normans, but were swiftly defeated by William the Conqueror. After surrendering to William, Edwin fled to Scotland but was betrayed by his own men and killed by the Normans, in 1071. His brother, Earl Morcar spent the remainder of his life in various Norman prisons. After Earl Edwin's death, the manor of Sutton Coldfield, along with the rest of the Mercian lands, became forfeit to the Norman Crown, and Sutton Chase became a Royal Forest.

1086
The Domesday Book

The Domesday Book of 1086 rates Sutton Coldfield as having eight hides; New Hall Estate being one of them, although it is not mentioned by name. A hide was an English unit of land measurement, originally intended to represent the amount of land sufficient to support a household. It was traditionally taken to be 120 acres but was also a measure of value and tax assessment, including obligations for food-rent, maintenance and repair of bridges and fortifications, and men to support the army.

1126
The Coming of the Earls of Warwick

In 1126 the lands on which New Hall was soon to be built came into the family of the Earls of Warwick, when Henry I exchanged his holdings around Sutton Coldfield with other property owned by Roger de Newburgh (otherwise known as Roger de Beaumont), the Norman Earl of Warwick. The Sutton Coldfield estates were to stay in the family of the Earls of Warwick - with two short breaks - until 1487.

2.

THE AGE OF THE MAGNATES: BUILDING NEW HALL, THE PLANTAGENETS AND THE WARS OF THE ROSES

1200
Building New Hall in the Age of the Plantagenets

At around the turn of the 12th century, the first mention of a house at the site of New Hall is recorded. Its position was determined by the abundance of water flowing around the site – there are seven fresh-water springs around the current location. Unsurprisingly, defence was a key factor in determining the position of manor houses at the time. England was still fairly unstable. The memory of the Anarchy (1138-53), the brutal 15 years civil war between the two royal claimants King Stephen and the Empress Matilda, daughter of King Henry I, would still have been fresh in people's minds. Nor was England completely peaceful under Matilda's Plantagenet descendants. More recently, King John, (King of England 1199-1216), had attempted a rebellion against his elder brother, King Richard the Lionheart, while King Richard was on Crusade in the Holy Land (1189-92). King John, once he inherited the throne from Richard the Lionheart in 1199, soon found himself facing conflict in Scotland, in France, in Ireland and Wales – and was excommunicated by the Pope over who had the right to appoint the Archbishop of Canterbury. Still to come, was the Barons' revolt (1215-17) against King John, sparked by his draconian tax demands, which resulted in the King's agreement to the Magna Carta in 1216, England's first Bill of Rights.

Therefore, the ability to put a moat around your house – using the natural water supply - must have seemed a sensible precaution and was clearly a deciding factor on where New Hall was built. The first structure seems to have been built of a grey-white stone, most of which still stands today with door and window openings being surrounded by ashlar – stone facing that has been chiselled flat. The house consisted of what is now the Great Hall and Dining Room, with bedrooms above. The moat surrounded the house – with only one access point – a draw-bridge that led to what is still the main front door today.

The reminder of the long association of the Earls of Warwick and New Hall can be found on the first-floor half landing of the main staircase, in the form of a carved figure on the newell of a bear and ragged staff. The bear has been a symbol of the House of Warwick since the Dark Ages, when the first Earl, Arth of Warwick - according to tradition, a Knight of the Round Table - adopted the Bear to represent him. The staff is attributed to the second Earl Morvid of Warwick who, according to the legend, added the staff after he overcame a giant, attacking him with a tree that had been plucked from the ground by its roots and stripped of its branches.

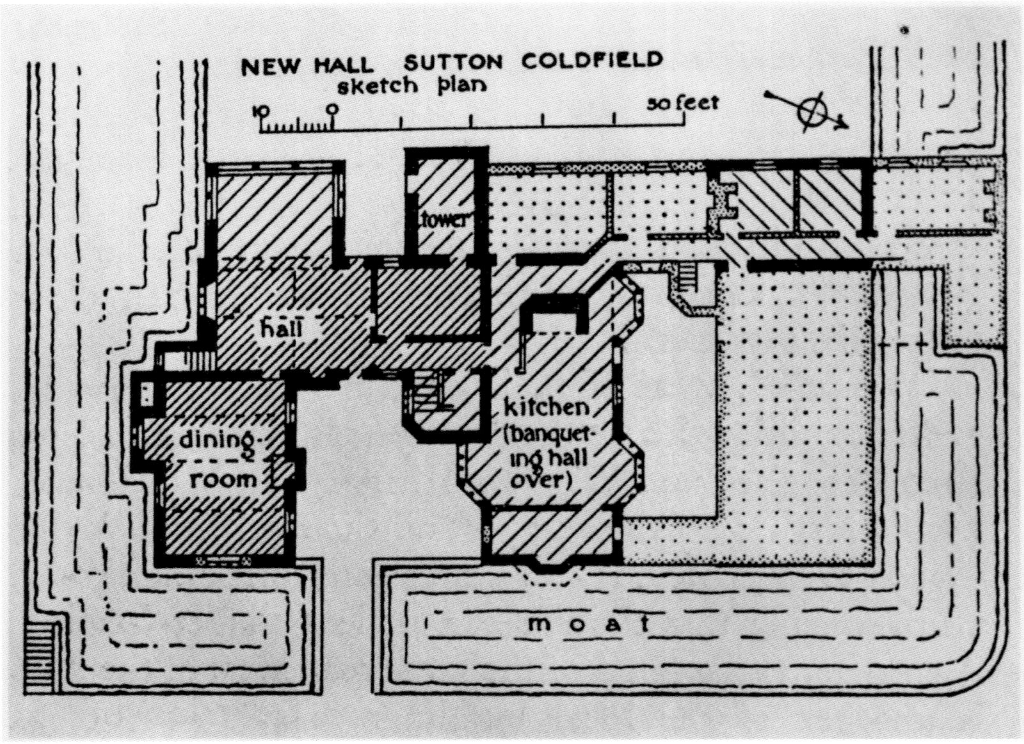

1327

In the early 14th century, the house went through a period of frequently changed ownership. In 1327, when Edward III came to the throne. New Hall is recorded as being owned by William de Sutton, a descendent of Guy, 10th Earl of Warwick, who had been one of main opponents of Edward III's father, Edward II. The estate then passed to Robert de Sutton, a merchant from Coventry, then passed back to Thomas Beauchamp, the 12th Earl of Warwick who, in 1341, is recorded as passing New Hall to Sir John Lizours of Fledbourough, in Nottinghamshire. Lizours was attached to the Courts of the Earls of Warwick. This is the first record of the name "New Hall".

1341–1437

The Lizours are named after the village near Rouen in France from where they originated. Following the Norman Conquest, they settled in Nottinghamshire. Sir John Lizours of Fledburgh entailed all his estates, including New Hall, a move which meant that only his family and direct heirs could inherit them. This means that there are no detailed records of who resided there until 1437, when Sir Richard Stanhope is recorded as having died there. At the time the New Hall estate spanned 407 acres. It appears that Richard Stanhope had been granted the right to live in New Hall for a life annuity of 12 pounds from Thomas Basset of Fledburgh, descendent of John Lizours. Richard Stanhope's daughter, Katherine, was married to Thomas Basset of Fledburgh's son William. After Thomas Basset's death, Katherine and William Basset continued to live at New Hall until William's death. Katherine then rented the estate for 21 years to William Deping of Sutton and Richard Ley of Maney.

In 1401, when Richard de Beauchamp became the Earl of Warwick, amongst his vast estates, were New Hall, the Manor of Sutton Coldfield and New Shipton farm. Richard de Beauchamp, like all the medieval Earls of Warwick, was a great magnate and warrior. He was one of the senior commanders in the English defence against Owen Glendower's Welsh Revolt (1400-1415). In 1403 Henry IV rewarded Earl Richard for his loyalty at the Battle of Shrewsbury by making him a Knight of the Garter. Earl Richard fought in France with King Henry V and, in 1422, was given the formidable task of forming a new government on behalf of the six-month old King Henry VI.

Through his two advantageous marriages and shrewd political and military manoeuvering, Earl Richard doubled his estates to become the wealthiest baron in England. As Earl of Warwick, Richard de Beauchamp made his main residence Caversham Castle, near Reading, but one of the first places he visited were his estates at Sutton to hunt and see to the business of his farms and the estates.

OPPOSITE: The medieval plan of New Hall's ground floor, showing the original Anglo-Saxon layout, where the moat surrounds the house, giving only one access point.

ON FOY

PREVIOUS PAGE: A view of the original Tudor front door across the drawbridge. Above are carved the Sacheverell coat of arms and the family motto in Latin 'En Bon Foy' – 'In Good Faith.'

1455–1485

The Wars of the Roses and Warwick the Kingmaker

During the 15th century, the Royal House of Plantagenet tore itself apart, with an on-going civil war between the rival cousins, the Houses of York and Lancaster. Known as the Wars of the Roses, or the Cousins' War, they are estimated to have claimed casualties well over 100,000, about 5.5% of the population of England at that time.

New Hall Estate not only sat at the heart of one of the most strategically and politically important regions in the country and, even more crucially, belonged to one of the most controversial figures: the great 15th century statesman, known as Warwick the Kingmaker – Richard Neville, 16th Earl of Warwick (1428-71), cousin of the Royal Dukes of York. Neville had become Earl of Warwick through the inheritance of his wife, Lady Anne Beauchamp, daughter of the last Beauchamp Earl of Warwick. Known as "the Kingmaker", Earl Richard of Warwick was the most powerful and controversial nobleman in England, and one of the richest. The King at the time, Henry VI of Lancaster, was mentally fragile and unsuited to rule. As a result, a period of civil war ripped through England, between the claimants of the rival Royal Houses of York and Lancaster. Warwick married his two daughters, Lady Isabel and Lady Anne Neville, to princes of both royal houses and changed sides accordingly. There were obviously huge economic advantages of having a great magnate as your patron, spending lavishly in your local economy. But if your overlord was a warlord like Warwick, fighting endless battles, then, in those dying days of feudalism, families and estates were still expected to provide troops and money to support his armies. So, although there are no specific records of New Hall for this time, the house, the estate and those who lived and worked there would have had their lives severely battered by the surrounding political storm.

Unfortunately for New Hall's owner, the Earl of Warwick, he switched sides once too often. His luck ran out in 1471 and he died at the Battle of Barnet, fighting for the – eventually unsuccessful – Lancastrian Henry VI, who was also the father-in-law of Warwick's daughter, Lady Anne. Henry VI's only son, Edward, Prince of Wales - Lady Anne's husband - had been killed the previous month at the Battle of Tewkesbury by the victorious Yorkists. Warwick's lands would normally have remained in possession of his widow, Countess Anne, who was after all the original Warwick heiress, but instead they were split between her two daughters: Isabel, who had been married since 1469 to her cousin, George, Duke of Clarence, younger brother of the Yorkist King Edward IV, and her sister, Lady Anne, the widowed Lancastrian Princess of Wales. Lady Anne was promptly married to the victorious Edward IV's youngest brother, Richard, Duke of Gloucester. After Clarence's execution for treason in 1478, Isabel's share was held in trust by the Crown for their 3-year-old son, Edward Plantagenet. As for Lady Anne, in 1483, her husband usurped the throne shortly after his brother's death, from his teenage nephew, Edward V, and was crowned Richard III. Queen Anne Neville died in 1485, shortly before her husband fell at the Battle of Bosworth, fighting against Henry Tudor, the next Lancastrian pretender. He then was King Henry VII, the first of the Tudor kings. Two years later, in 1487, Henry VII gave the vast Warwick lands back to the ageing Countess of Warwick, who promptly, and shrewdly, immediately returned them to the Tudor Crown, and that included the estate of New Hall. New Hall was now the property of the King.

ABOVE TOP ROW: One of the many eyecatching historical features of New Hall are the carved newel posts, created by the Sacheverells, on the Tudor staircase. From left to right is the Lion of England holding the Sacheverell coat of arms, the Bear and Ragged Staff, the emblem of the Earls of Warwick and the Sacheverell Goat, *statant* (still or sitting).

BOTTOM ROW LEFT TO RIGHT: The Sacheverell Goat, *passant*, the Lion of England and the Gibbons family Dragon (also seen at the entrance to what is now the reception area at New Hall).

3.

THE TUDOR ROSE, NEW MEN AND THE REFORMATION

THE TUDOR ROSE, NEW MEN AND THE REFORMATION

1525
The Gibbons Family and the Reformation

By 1525 Henry VIII had been on the throne for sixteen years and England was relatively stable. It is in this year that there is the first record of a William Gibbons living at New Hall. The Tudor monarchs reigned over a time of enormous social change in England, combined with more than a century of unprecedented peace. The new ownership of New Hall reflects that change. The Tudors' policy was to humble the old over-mighty feudal warlords, like the Earls of Warwick, and reward new men, loyal primarily to the regime, many of whom were merchants or lawyers - people today we would recognize as businessmen. They were encouraged and enabled to make fortunes. The Reformation, the vast lands and wealth redistributed through the dissolution of the monasteries, the relative stability, all brought new opportunities. William Gibbons was to take advantage of these changes.

1465–1554
Bishop John Vesey, Henry VIII and Sutton Coldfield's Tudor Rose

Bishop Vesey was a local boy made good, who returned Sutton Coldfield and New Hall to the political significance they had enjoyed under the medieval Earls of Warwick. Bishop John Vesey was one of the most influential figures in England at that time. Bishop of Exeter, Vesey was a powerful player in the court Henry VIII, tutor to King Henry's daughter, Mary and a close friend of the King's. He was also the brother of William Gibbons' wife, Agnes. New Hall once again would host figures of national importance. Bishop John Vesey was born John Harman, at Moor Farm in Sutton Coldfield, in around 1465. Vesey/Harman was the eldest son of William Harman, a minor squire. Young John grew up during the Wars of the Roses, one of the most turbulent periods in English history, in which Sutton's feudal overlord, the Earl of Warwick, was one of the major players.

According to John Vesey's tombstone in Holy Trinity Church in Sutton, he had a younger brother and two sisters, including, Agnes, wife to William Gibbons of New Hall. Very little is known about Bishop Vesey's early years but they were clearly difficult. Some historians believe that when his father died in 1470 - the same year that the Yorkist King Edward IV fled to France and the Lancastrian Henry VI was briefly restored to the throne - John was forced to take responsibility for his family, as the Wars of the Roses raged around them. If John had been born in 1452, he would have been 18 when his father died; or if, as other historians believe, he had been born in 1465, he would have been only 13. Either way he was young, and hardship gave him the skills to become a wily political player.

Having Warwick the Kingmaker as your Lord of the Manor had certainly had upsides and downsides. Because of feudal obligations, Warwick was able to place heavy demands on the local gentry such as the Harmans, for both financial and military support. However, the influence and political significance of a man of Warwick's stature had also brought huge prosperity to the region. But when Warwick was killed in battle in 1471, Bishop Vesey's home town lost its influential patron. As a result, Sutton entered a period of huge economic and social decline. The region, like the rest of England, was also dealing with the impact of years of civil war on society: young men had gone to fight in the wars, leaving farmland with nobody to work it. Food was scarce and many locals lived in the grip of poverty.

ABOVE: Moor Hall , the birthplace of John Harman, later Bishop Vesey, is now at 29, Moor Hall Drive, Sutton Coldfield, and beautifully restored. Pevsner described it as a sandstone house of the sixteenth century, perhaps earlier'.

It is thought that young John, not long after his father's death, was sent to live with his relatives, the Veseys of Chimney, in Oxfordshire. This would have allowed him to study and receive the education that later won him a place at Magdalene College, Oxford. It would also account for his name change from Harman to Vesey. While at Oxford, John Vesey got to know his fellow Magdalene student, Thomas Wolsey. Cardinal Wolsey, as he became, would go on to become one of the great statesmen of England, chief advisor to King Henry VIII, the builder of Hampton Court. John Vesey followed his friend Wolsey to London and joined the Royal Household. It was under Wolsey's patronage that John was appointed the Bishop of Exeter in 1509, shortly after Henry VIII was crowned king.

Bishop Vesey, like Wolsey, was known to be a confidante of King Henry VIII, from Henry's earliest years on the throne. Vesey became a powerful figure in both the Church and national politics. He travelled widely throughout England, before returning to Sutton in 1518, in his late fifties, to take up permanent residence. As the lands of the Earl of Warwick had become forfeit to the Crown by the end of the Wars of the Roses, Henry VIII was Sutton and New Hall's feudal overlord. The King granted his friend some land at "Le Moreheath" or Moor Heath, close to John's family home, on which Vesey built a new house called Moor Hall.

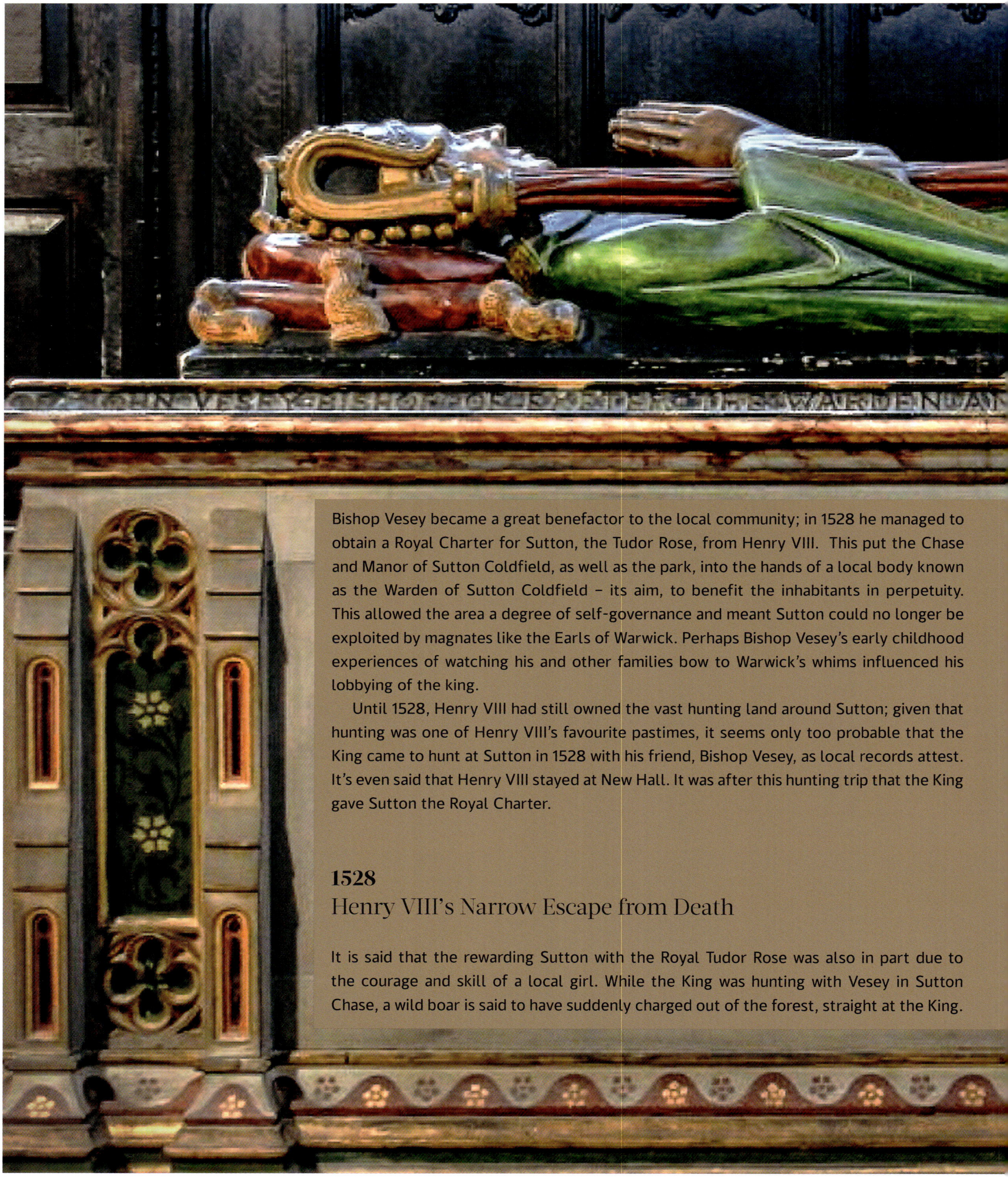

Bishop Vesey became a great benefactor to the local community; in 1528 he managed to obtain a Royal Charter for Sutton, the Tudor Rose, from Henry VIII. This put the Chase and Manor of Sutton Coldfield, as well as the park, into the hands of a local body known as the Warden of Sutton Coldfield – its aim, to benefit the inhabitants in perpetuity. This allowed the area a degree of self-governance and meant Sutton could no longer be exploited by magnates like the Earls of Warwick. Perhaps Bishop Vesey's early childhood experiences of watching his and other families bow to Warwick's whims influenced his lobbying of the king.

Until 1528, Henry VIII had still owned the vast hunting land around Sutton; given that hunting was one of Henry VIII's favourite pastimes, it seems only too probable that the King came to hunt at Sutton in 1528 with his friend, Bishop Vesey, as local records attest. It's even said that Henry VIII stayed at New Hall. It was after this hunting trip that the King gave Sutton the Royal Charter.

1528
Henry VIII's Narrow Escape from Death

It is said that the rewarding Sutton with the Royal Tudor Rose was also in part due to the courage and skill of a local girl. While the King was hunting with Vesey in Sutton Chase, a wild boar is said to have suddenly charged out of the forest, straight at the King.

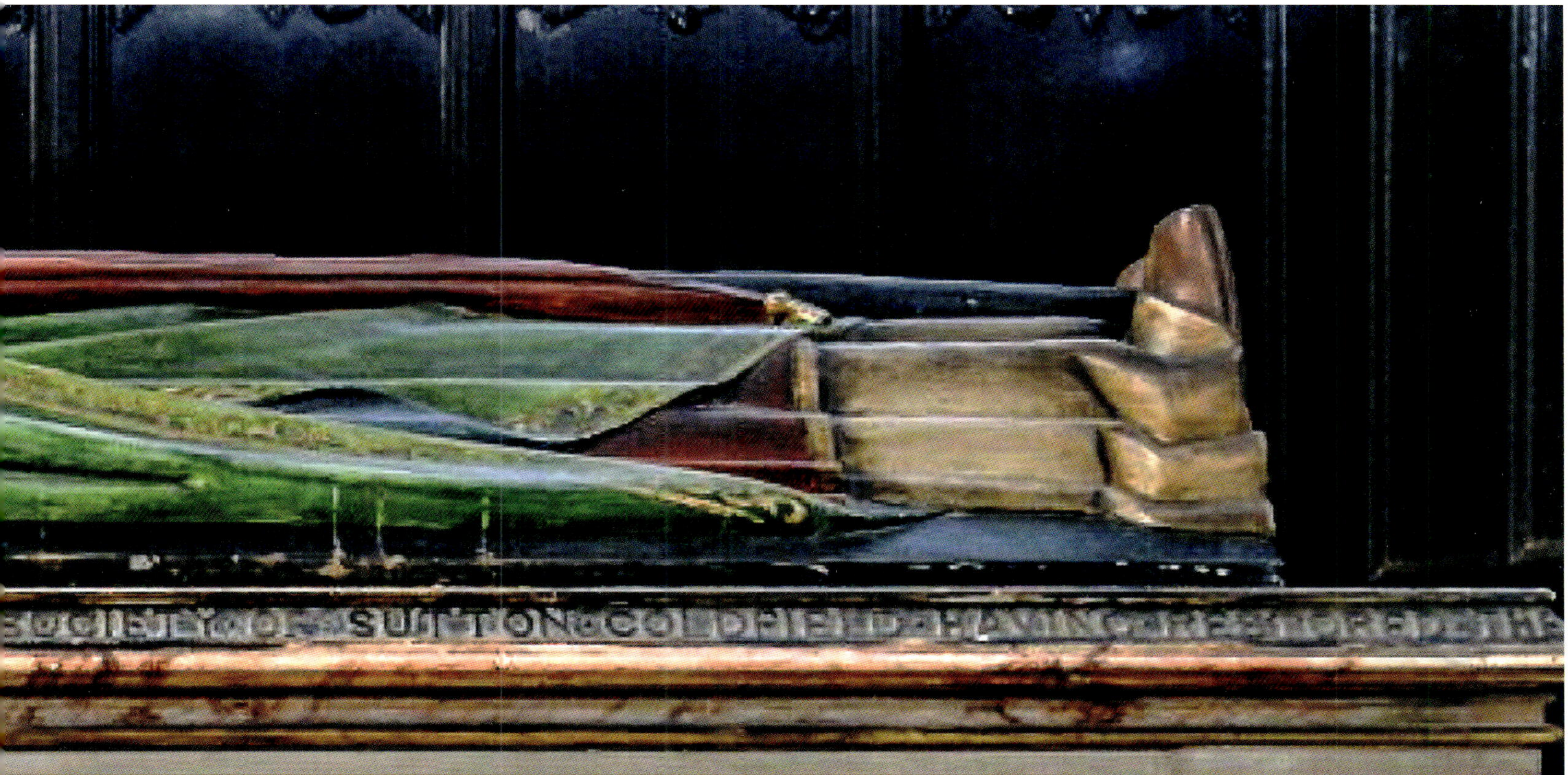

The King had hardly time to move, expecting death any second, but suddenly an arrow shot out of the trees. It killed the boar stone-dead. When the king asked for the person who'd saved his life to come forward, a ragged young woman appeared shyly from the woods. She was the daughter of local gentry who had been dispossessed of their lands. Sutton Coldfield was rewarded with the Royal Charter – and the girl's family's lands were returned to them.

The very first Warden of Sutton Coldfield was Bishop Vesey's brother-in-law, William Gibbons of New Hall, a title inherited by his son Thomas, on William's death in 1542. Vesey survived the fall of his benefactor Wolsey in 1529, continuing to prosper under Thomas Cromwell and after Cromwell's fall. Vesey kept his Bishopric until 1551, by which time Henry VIII's much more devoutly Protestant son, Edward VI, was on the throne; Vesey's opposition to the Reformation finally caught up with him. Edward VI forced Vesey to resign his title of Bishop, in exchange for a pension of £485 a year – about £150,000 a year today. But when Vesey's former pupil, Henry VIII's daughter, Queen Mary, acceded to the throne in 1553, she reinstated her old tutor as Bishop of Exeter. Vesey, now a very old man – being either 101 or 88 depending on what date of birth you believe – died a year later.

Above: Bishop Vesey's tomb at Holy Trinity Church, Sutton Coldfield. It is the only monumental effigy of a bishop in Warwickshire. His robes are pre-Reformation, denoting his return to Catholicism.

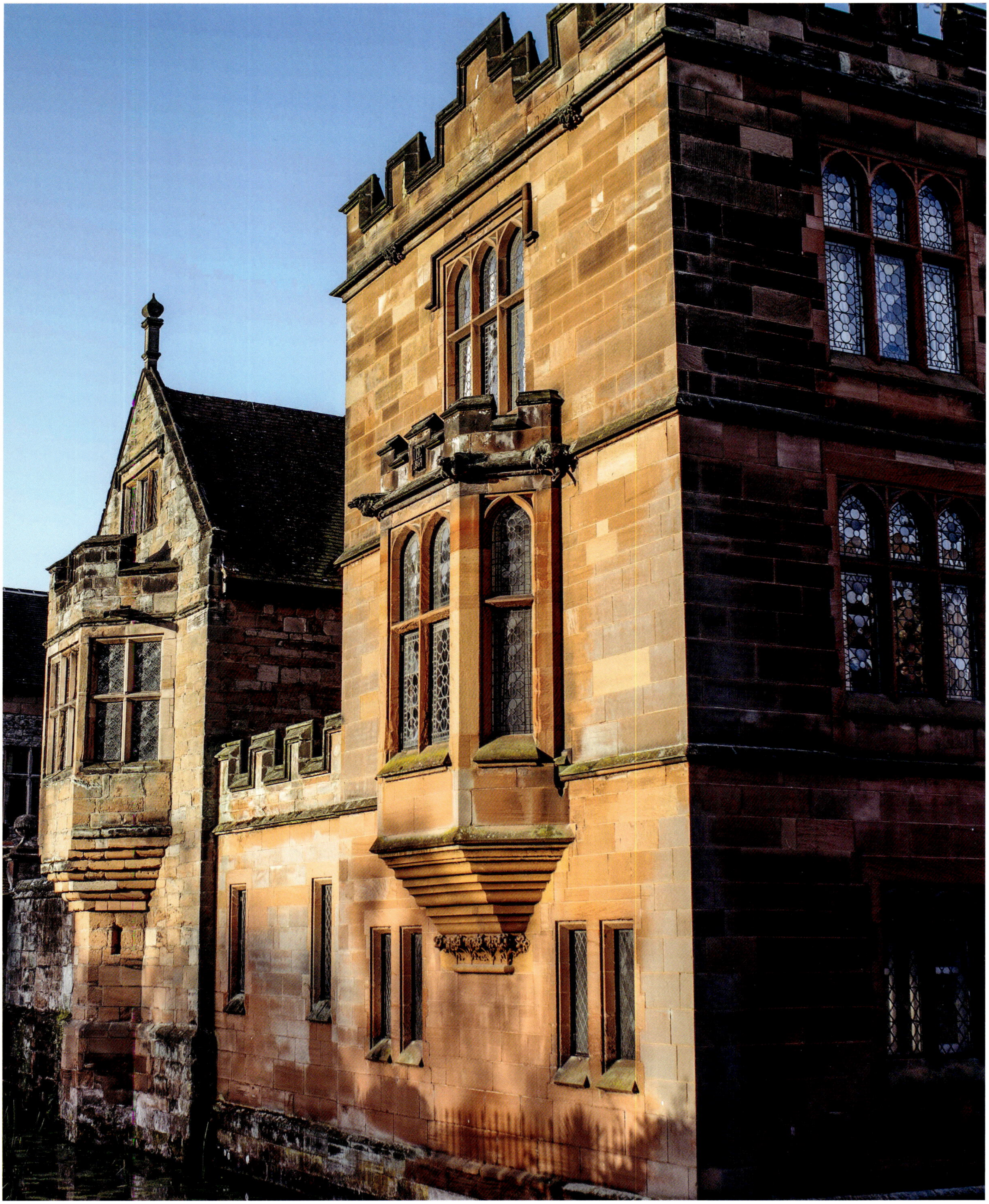

LEFT: The North Wing was added to New Hall in 1542, built in red sandstone rather than the grey ashlar of the original Anglo-Saxon keep. Mullioned windows were added to the extended Great Chamber.

1542
Thomas Gibbons rebuilds New Hall

It was Thomas Gibbons, Bishop Vesey's nephew and William Gibbons' son, who started rebuilding New Hall. Thanks to the unprecedented political stability in England, this was the first time for centuries that landowners could think about building houses for beauty and comfort, rather than for defence. It was the very start of the era of the great English Country House. New Hall stands at the forefront of this new age.

Thomas Gibbons had become, by all accounts, a very rich man. Thomas also married two heiress, Eleanor Arden of Oxfordshire, and after her death, Elizabeth Pierpoint, whose family owned wharves in London. New Hall was just one of Thomas's estates. Being closely related to Bishop Vesey also made the Gibbons family ideally placed to take financial advantage of the redistribution of church assets that took place during the dissolution of the monasteries. In 1542, Thomas added the North Wing, including the Great Chamber, to match the style of the existing L-shaped building, but in a red sandstone rather than the greyer stone of the medieval house. The old Great Hall was extended, and a large Tudor chimney added to the South Side, of which the base remains; the chimney now forms the base of a tower that was added later. Mullioned windows were added to the South and East facades, along with ornate gables to the front façade, where the property was still accessed by the bridge over the moat.

In 1559, five years after the death of his uncle, Bishop Vesey, Thomas Gibbons purchased the right to appoint the clergy to Sutton Parish Church. At the time such a practice was considered a valuable investment, as it gave landowners considerable power in the community. But things were about to go wrong for Thomas GIbbons: in 1581, Gibbons is recorded as appearing before the fearsome Star Chamber Court in Westminster to answer charges of wrongful appropriation of Church land. His right to appoint clergy was rescinded. The fact that his case was heard at the Star Chamber shows how powerful the Gibbons family had become – the Star Chamber was specifically to try people whom ordinary courts and judges might be afraid to convict.

Thomas Gibbons died shortly afterwards in 1586 and his son, another Thomas Gibbons inherited the New Hall estate. Perhaps the family lost money after the Star Chamber judgement. Whatever the reason, Thomas Gibbons II did not want to live in the Hall. Instead he rented it out to a Percy Willoughby of Nottingham. After the lease expired, Thomas sold New Hall to his brother William Gibbons II, who died shortly afterwards. William's wife, Mary continued to live at New Hall until her death in 1608, leaving four sons, none of whom appeared to want to live there.

4.

THE SACHEVERELLS: ALCHEMY, INCEST AND THE RISE OF THE LANDED GENTRY AND THE TRAVAILS OF THE ROYAL STUARTS

1612
The Coming of the Sacheverells and the Mystery of the Priest Hole

Henry Sacheverell of Morley and Callow, in Derbyshire, purchased New Hall officially in 1612. The Sacheverells were one of the most ancient and influential families to have owned New Hall. The Sacheverells claimed to descend from knights from the Norman village of Sault Chevreuil du Tronchet who had come to England with William the Conqueror. They were typical of the families of landed gentry who became increasingly prominent after the Tudors broke the power of the great feudal magnates. Although the Sacheverells' tenure of New Hall was relatively short, their political leanings and the guests they had to stay at New Hall were historically significant.

Henry Sacheverell had three or four children by his first wife Jane, but they separated in 1593. Henry later settled in Leicestershire with his mistress, Elizabeth Kayes, with whom he had two illegitimate children; one of these was Sacheverell's son Valens, born in 1604. Henry was a Recusant Catholic, adhering to the Old Faith; he refused to attend Church of England services. Unfortunately for Sacheverell, Henry VIII's second daughter, Queen Elizabeth I (who reigned from 1558-1603) had passed harsh laws against Catholics – although it was understandable, considering the Pope had declared Elizabeth illegitimate, and Catholics regarded her cousin Mary Queen of Scots as the rightful Queen of England. As a result, Catholics were liable to heavy taxation by the Crown for refusing to adhere to the new Protestant faith. To avoid the tax, Henry Sacheverell decided to buy estates for his children. He bought New Hall in Valens's name from the Gibbons family. The "Livery of Seisin" ceremony was carried out in 1612 and Valens attended the ceremony, to verify the property's new owner.

Because of Sacheverell's Catholicism, the Priest hole in one of the upper bedrooms of the older part of New Hall probably dates from this period. The door leads to a small, cramped space in which Catholic Priests would have hidden from the Queen's men during her reign. Households that harboured such priests, who were normally Jesuits, had similar religious and political leanings to Henry Sacheverell. The priests, if found, were put on public trial, and often executed by the brutal method of hanging drawing and quartering.

1612
En Bon Foy and New Hall's alterations

As a Catholic, Henry Sacheverell would have had no prospects at court of Elizabeth I, or indeed that of her heir, her Scottish raised, Protestant cousin James I. As a result, he concentrated his energies and money on improving New Hall and his son, Valens, continued his father's work.

In the original part of the old hall, the Sacheverells put in several oak studded doors – above which were carved the family motto "En Bon Foy" meaning "In Good Faith". Above another door, they had the figure of a goat, their family crest, engraved. The former staircase was elaborated and embellished with heraldic beasts, the Great Chamber was enlarged, and bay windows added. The opulent interiors of the old part of New Hall seem predominantly to come from Henry Sacheverell's work, including putting the oak panelling in the corridors, downstairs Dining Hall and upstairs in the Great Chamber. The pilasters on either side of the fireplace in the Dining Hall are decorated with a fern motif which is mirrored in the pilasters on either side of the Great Chamber's fireplace.

The frieze work in the Great Chamber is embellished with sea monsters and the Sacheverell's goat family crest. The ornate plasterwork ceiling in the Great Chamber is decorated with suns, small, embellished scrolls and fruit pendants. The Sacheverell Coat of Arms is on display in the middle of the ceiling as well as on the stained-glass bay windows. The building was extended north. Just beyond the moat, a two-story stone building was erected, in which the size and windows suggest it was a chapel, presumably a private place of Catholic worship.

1620
Valens Sacheverell Comes into his Inheritance

Henry Sacheverell died in 1620 and, by 1628, his son Valens and his young wife, Anne, had taken up residence in New Hall. With his inheritance, Valens became a man of assured position rather than an illegitimate child. He was therefore able to marry Anne, the daughter of Sir George Devereux of Sheldon Hall, and niece to powerful and well-connected William Devereux, fifth Viscount Hereford. Hereford was ancient nobility, who had adapted and evolved under the Tudors; he was a cousin not only of the old Plantagenet kings, but also of Queen Elizabeth's powerful, fallen favourite, Walter Devereux, the great Earl of Essex, whom Elizabeth had executed in 1576. Valens and Anne had six children, but only two survived – George, their son and heir was born in 1632, and a daughter, also called Anne, was born in 1629. Valens was the first owner of New Hall to register the births of his two children at the Parish Church of Holy Trinity.

The Yew Tree Walk

The Archery lawn extends beyond the moat at New Hall, and beyond it lies the Yew Tree Walk, a tunnel of around 18 ancient yews leading to a circle of trees. It is unclear when the Yew Tree Walk was first planted but was likely during the Sacheverells' time. Yew wood was excellent for making bows used in archery and for fighting in battle. The yew trees were planted to ensure that both members of the household and passing soldiers had access to a steady supply of good, sturdy long bows, as well as shady place to walk.

1645
War again – Roundheads, Cavaliers and Charles II

Between 1642 and 1651 England once again descended into Civil War. This time the battle was between Oliver Cromwell's Parliamentarian Roundheads and the Royalists Cavaliers who were loyal to King Charles I. Valens, given his Catholic father and well-connected wife was, inevitably, a cavalier. He allowed New Hall to be used to house Royalist soldiers and supporters, before Charles I's defeat and his execution in 1649. Valens is even supposed to have sheltered Charles II for a night, when the young King was fleeing from England to France, after the Royalists' defeat at the Battle of Worcester, in 1651. The fugitive King, with £1000 price on his head - £250,000 today - was certainly known to have spent several nights in the area, during his month on the run. Like many cavaliers, Valens paid the price for backing the losing side: in 1645 it is recorded that Valens was charged with "compounding for delinquency in deserting his house for enemy quarters" for which he was fined the sum of 542 pounds, over £130,000 today.

Valens Sacheverell died between 1655 and 1660. There is no record of Valen's burial in the local Parish registers or graveyards, so he may have died in battle, or even have gone into in exile on the Continent, like Charles II and so many other Royalists.

1660
George Sacheverell – The Alchemist of New Hall

By 1660, the year Charles II was restored to the throne, George Sacheverell, Valens' son, had inherited New Hall. George also inherited an estate at Callow, in Derbyshire, from his uncle, Jacinth Sacheverell. George Sacheverell was widely known to be eccentric and opinionated. He remained devoted to the Stuart cause, becoming, in later life, a firm Jacobite; he became an avid supporter of King James II, Charles II's Catholic brother and heir. George had studied at Oriel College in Oxford, just after the defeat of the Royalist Cause – a college with strong Cavalier links: King Charles I's headquarters had been based in Oxford and Oriel College was the home of the King's Privy Council. George Sacheverell, in later life, was elected a Fellow of Oriel College; Oriel still owns a silver salver and tankard engraved with the Sacheverell Arms which were presented to them on George's death. The College of Arms also granted George the right to bear the Sacheverell Arms - with an additional "Border Gules" a red border - a right which had been withheld from his father, Valens, because of Valens' illegitimacy. George Sacheverell married twice – first to Lucy Danet, and then to Mary Wilson who survived him. There were no surviving children from either marriage. And neither marriage seems to have been very happy. Certainly, George has gone down in family history as a very troubled man.

1689
Incest and Forbidden Love on a Window Pane

There are many rumours about the nature of George's relationship with his sister Anne – certainly he was broken-hearted after her death. Anne lived in Sutton Coldfield, with her husband, Charles Chadwick despite Charles owning extensive estates in Staffordshire. Anne Chadwick died young, shortly after her mother's death, in 1688. George Sacheverell then suffered a nervous breakdown. He is said to have been confined to New Hall for long periods. There is a tradition that George and his sister Anne had an incestuous relationship – although there is no hard evidence to prove this. These stories stem partly from love-lorn poems and quotations found etched - mainly in Latin - on panes of glass in the Great Chamber and in other rooms in the house The mullioned windows were probably installed by George's grandfather, but the writings on them are clearly signed by George Sacheverell, and dated to 1689 and 1690. They were probably etched with a diamond ring. One thing that is clear from the etchings that – incest or not - George was in love with someone that he should not have been and was a sad and deeply troubled soul.

ETCHINGS ON THE WINDOWS IN THE PRINCESS ELIZABETH SUITE AT NEW HALL

Omnia perdidimus tantummodo vita relicta est
Praebeat ut sensum materniamque malis.
G Sacheverell Apr 29 '90
"I have lost all, only life remains so that it may offer both sensation and material for pain" Taken from Ovid, Letters from the Black Sea.

ETCHINGS IN THE GREAT CHAMBER

Malo me fortuna peniteat quam victoria pudeat
I prefer that I regret my fortune then be ashamed of my victory

Alchemy, the Devil's Work and Gunpowder

There are, however, local traditions and reports in various poetry books that one of the Sacheverells practiced alchemy, the art of changing physical matter through magic. The clue that it was the childless George comes from a line in the poem called "Sacheverell's Warning", which describes the alchemist Sacheverell as "last of his race".

Sullen Sacheverell, last of the race,
Of New Hall's fair lands to be master,
Leave magic and alchemy, fly from this place,
Thou art warned of impending disaster."

Another poem, "The Alchemist of New Hall", describes visitation from a demon; this shows that some people locally, at least, must have thought Sacheverell to be in a league with the devil. On the other hand, he may have just been an amateur chemist, experimenting with a new form of gunpowder.

George kept a locked, secret study at New Hall, where he was rumoured to practice his alchemy. The exact location of this room is not certain but when the passage, known as the Screen, at the side of the Great Hall was removed, an oak-panelled room was discovered. It could have been George's secret study. It is unsurprising, then, given the rumours of George's satanism, alchemy and forlorn, incestuous love, that many of the inhabitants of New Hall report having strange experiences in the Great Chamber: hearing ghostly footsteps following them around the room, and the Great Chamber being engulfed by an unnatural chill. Despite his mental and spiritual confusion, George was said to be an exemplary Justice of Sutton for many years. He was known for being God-fearing and kind to the poor. In his will it was stated that, after his funeral, ten pounds was to be split amongst the poor of the Parish, with an annual distribution of bread worth five pounds a year - about £1000 and £500 today. George was also granted permission to build a family vault in the Parish Church of Holy Trinity in 1706 and on this engraved a flattering tribute to himself - stating that he was known for "affability, politeness and serious study who during the Civil War followed arts and Poetry not the war".

1688
The Glorious Revolution, Jacobites v Hanoverians, Tories v Whigs

Although non-military, George Sacheverell, with his family history of Catholicism and support for the House of Stuart, became involved in the great political controversy of his time. Charles II had died without legitimate issue in 1685 and his brother, James II, had inherited the throne. James II was Catholic, unlike his subjects. As his father Charles I had, James believed in the Divine Right of Kings. In late 1685, James II, took on Parliament – dismissing Parliament in 1685 for refusing to pass measures removing legal restrictions on Catholics and non-conformist Protestants, which led to widespread outrage. As James II had no son, and his two daughters from his first marriage, Mary and Anne, were Protestants and married to Protestant princes, a Protestant future for the Crown seemed secure.Things started to go badly wrong for James II when, in June 1688, his Catholic second wife, Queen Mary of Modena, gave birth to a boy, James Edward Stuart, a Catholic Prince of Wales. It looked as if Great Britain would now be ruled by a Catholic dynasty. Leading English Protestant politicians invited James II's son-in-law, the Protestant and Dutch Prince William of Orange, who was married to James' eldest daughter, Mary, to become King. The excuse was that the baby Prince James was a changeling, smuggled into his mother's bed "in a warming pan", a story that was unlikely to be true, given that the poor Queen had given birth surrounded by a gaggle of reputable witnesses. James II, however, was forced to flee to France with his young Catholic family. This became known as the Glorious Revolution. Prince William and his wife Mary became joint King and Queen of England. Their supporters were known as Whigs. The Tories tendedto support the exiled King James. George Sacheverell, unsurprisingly given his family historyand personal cussedness,was a Tory and soon George would be given an opportunity to show his allegiance.

1709
Dr Henry Sacheverell – an Unfortunate Friendship

PREVIOUS PAGE: The window seat in the Upper Hall provides a quiet place to read, with Charles Chadwick's stained glass window throwing beads of sunlight across the ancient panelling.

Dr Henry Sacheverell was a firebrand High Anglican, Jacobite cleric, preaching at the start of the 18th century. Despite his name, Dr Henry was not related to the Sacheverells of New Hall; his family originated from Dorset, from a village called Cheverall. Dr Henry, however, made the acquaintance of the fiercely Jacobite George Sacheverell, and managed to convince him that they were related. He soon became George's firm favourite, an honoured guest at New Hall. Because George owned an estate at Callow, in Derbyshire, he was appointed High Sheriff of the county, with the right to nominate a Chaplain. George chose the then increasingly infamous Dr Henry. England at the start of the 18th century was facing considerable unrest. A protracted war with France had resulted in a huge rise in the cost of living. Food was scarce and daily commodities like candles and fuel for cooking increased in price. Against this backdrop, political feelings ran high.

In 1709, Dr Henry Sacheverell preached a sermon at St Paul's Cathedral in London entitled "The Perils of False Brethren in Church and State". This wasa personal attack against the Prime Minister Lord Godolphin, a Tory who was now supporting the Whig cause – as well as the Lord Mayor and Aldermen of London. The speech was printed and circulated widely – who condemned the sermon. Dr Sacheverell was charged with Sedition and impeached.

Queen Anne Graces Dr Henry's Trial

Dr Henry Sacheverell's trial took place at Westminster Hall. Somewhat surprisingly, Queen Anne attended Dr Henry's trial every day for three weeks to show her support for his views. Enormously fat, the Queen arrived every day in a sedan chair, carried by her long-suffering footmen. Queen Anne 's views were shared by the majority of the population, whose backing for Dr Henry's cause came from the distribution of pamphlets and requests for prayers on his behalf at Churches throughout London. Sir Christopher Wren was called upon to build extra seating at the trial for the sheer numbers who attended. The Tories were fully supportive of Henry's position. He was, however, found guilty and suspended from preaching for three years. The offending sermons were ordered to be burnt on the steps of the Royal Exchange.

The light sentence passed on Dr Henry only served to motivate his supporters and increase his popularity. This played a considerable part in the defeat of the Whigs at the next General Election, returning the Tories to power. In 1711, during the three years in which Dr Henry was banned from preaching, Dr Henry is said to have come to live at New Hall, with his patron George. Queen Anne died in early August 1714, after suffering a series of strokes. Her successor, her Protestant second cousin, George I, the German Elector of Hanover, landed in Greenwich on September 18th 1714. The Jacobites, including George and Henry, were adamant that the rightful heir to the throne was James Stuart, Anne's Catholic half-brother. But the Act of Settlement of 1701 forbade an English monarch from being a Catholic.

On the 20th of October 1714, a week before George's coronation, it is likely that Henry was staying at New Hall when he preached an inflammatory sermon to a congregation of over 200 Birmingham Jacobites in Sutton Coldfield Parish Church. When the congregation left the Church, they ran riot through the town, attacking government buildings and disturbing the peace. The Whig Government responded by putting Henry under house arrest at New Hall. He languished there, forgotten by his supporters and ignored by the government.

1715
George Sacheverell Changes his Will

Dr Henry, meanwhile, had managed to convince an aging George Sacheverell that they were related by blood, despite the tenuous links. On 5 May 1715, shortly before his death, George – who had no children of his own - made a will leaving half of Callow, his Derbyshire estate, to Dr Henry. Dr Henry was also, according to George's will, to be paid fifty pounds for "preaching my funeral sermon in Sutton Church". George died shortly afterwards, on 18 May 1715, at the age of 83. Just a month after George's death, Dr Henry married George's widow, Mary, fourteen years his senior. In George's will, not only did Mary inherit George's "chariot, the two coach horses and harness, the bed and furniture of the white chamber and eight pictures", but Mary also retained the right to live at New Hall for life. Her new husband Dr Henry, having lived there since 1711, remained at New Hall with Mary as her husband. As a result of all this, Dr Henry became a reasonably wealthy man, eventually buying a house in Highgate, North London. He died at Highgate, in 1723 after suffering a fall. As for George, his body was buried in the Sacheverell family vault he had built at Holy Trinity Church, in Sutton Coldfield. When dry rot was discovered in 1965, during the renovations, five lead coffins were found, containing the remains of both the Sacheverell and Chadwick families.

5.

THE CHADWICKS – A CENTURY OF RESPECTABILITY, THE RISE OF EMPIRE AND THE INDUSTRIAL REVOLUTION

1715
The Sensible Chadwicks

George Sacheverell died childless in 1715, leaving no direct heirs. However, his beloved sister Anne Chadwick had had a family with her husband, Charles Chadwick, and a thriving brood of grandchildren. Charles Chadwick was himself a wealthy landowner. His family came from Healey, in Lancashire and, like the Sacheverells, could trace Norman descent and still owned the estates they had been granted by the Conqueror. Charles Chadwick, on his mother's side, came from a Staffordshire family called Mavesyn, who traced their line back to the Sire de Rosny, one of the knights who fought for William the Conqueror at the Battle of Hastings. After the conquest, de Rosny was rewarded with the lordship of the manor and land around Ridware in Staffordshire. De Rosny, according to local tradition, built a castle, changed his name to Malvoisin – literally Bad Neighbour - and promptly started attacking the neighbouring landowners. This proved to be rather lucrative, and the bellicose Malvoisin/de Rosny built up large estates. Malvoisin, over the ages, turned into Mavesyn, and the village became known as Mavesyn Ridware. Charles Chadwick became High Sheriff of Derbyshire in 1709, and later, in 1719, High Sheriff of Staffordshire.

George Sacheverell and his brother-in-law Charles Chadwick did not get on – Charles Chadwick was as ardent a Whig as George Sacheverell was a Tory – but whether the estrangement was because of their political differences or the rumours of George's incestuous love for Charles' wife Anne, is not known. This breach might have contributed to George leaving his widow, Mary, the right to New Hall for life, and half his Callow estate to Dr Henry Sacheverell. By the time George Sacheverell died, however, his brother-in-law Charles Chadwick had been dead since 1697. So George left New Hall, its estate, and the remaining half of Callow to Charles Chadwick and Anne's grandson, also called Charles Chadwick (II), who had been born in 1705, and was only 10 years old. In his will, George severely reproached Charles' grandfather for disagreeing with his politics and just to drive the point home, George made Charles Chadwick II's inheritance conditional on taking the Sacheverell name within 12 months of his 21st Birthday. New Shipton Farm - part of the estate - was left to George's niece, Anne's daughter Catherine, who was married to another landowner, Ralph Foyer of Hints in Staffordshire. Charles Chadwick II did not move into New Hall until after his great-aunt Mary Sacheverell's death in 1729. He was in the prime of his youth, aged 24. However, it is clear money was an issue for young Charles, because he soon took out a mortgage against New Hall with a Francis Horton of Wolverhampton for the sum of £1040 – about £250,000 today. This may have been to pay for his marriage to his fiancée, Anna Maria Brearly.

1745
The Jacobite Rebellion, Butcher Cumberland and the Ghost of the Bodiless Head

In 1745, the threat of civil war once again loomed over the United Kingdom – and its shadow touched New Hall. Bonnie Prince Charlie, the son of the Stuart pretender to the throne, grandson of the exiled King James II, landed in Scotland in July 1745. He had only seven men and little money or weapons, but the Highland clans came out for their prince. Facing little opposition, the Prince and his army took Scotland, and got as far south as Derby in December, before his Highland Chieftains, spooked by being so far from home and the lack of support from the English Jacobites and Tories, turned back north.

In April 1746, at the Battle of Culloden, near Inverness, Bonnie Prince Charlie's army, was conclusively defeated by the British army led by George II's son, the Duke of Cumberland – whose barbarous cruelty in the reprisals after Culloden, earned him the nickname Butcher Cumberland. It is not known whether Charles Chadwick was a Jacobite like his Sacheverell forbears but there are no reports of the Chadwicks offering their support for the Prince. Butcher Cumberland had his suspicions, for in 1745, as Cumberland's army was heading north, it passed close to New Hall. The Duke's advance party was lost, and asked directions from a local. Unfortunately, the man had a cleft palate, and the soldiers could not understand his reply. Apparently thinking the man was a spy, the officer had him executed. The poor man's head was chopped off, and "carried in triumph" on a halberd to nearby New Shipton, where it was chucked into an oak tree. When the tree was chopped down in 1827, the man's skull rolled free. Ever since, allegedly, his bodiless head can be seen drifting across New Hall estate, towards the place where his corpse was dumped, hoping to be made whole again.

1779
Death by Burning Bonnet

Charles took his great-uncle George's name as required and became Charles Sacheverell Chadwick. but had no children. New Hall was passed his younger, unmarried sister, Dorothy, who also inherited Callow and Mavesyn Ridgware on her brother's death in 1779. Dorothy happily took on the ownership but she came to a somewhat unexpected end: she died in 1784 after setting her bonnet alight with a candle while counting out money to give to a charity. New Hall passed to her uncle, Ralph Floyer, who already owned New Shipton Farm. This was only for his lifetime, with a proviso that New Hall would then pass to yet another Charles Chadwick (1753-1829), this one the son of Dorothy's half-brother, Colonel John de Healey Chadwick (1720-1800). John, who had married an heiress, was a wealthy man. His family's main residence was Healey Hall in Lancashire.

1793
Beautifying New Hall – The Fat Days of the Landed Gentry

When Ralph Floyer died in 1793, Charles Chadwick III, newly married to his wife, Frances, then took possession of New Hall and Callow. This was a great century for the Landed Gentry. The powerful - sometimes psychotic - feudal warlords of the Middle Ages were long gone, as was the terrifying confusion of the 17th century Civil War and the threat of Jacobite uprisings. England was peaceful; trade and commerce had become the economic drivers rather than warfare and loot. Thanks to the spread of the British influence throughout the globe, opportunities for making money in international trade were rapidly growing. There had also been a revolution in the 18th century in agriculture and the industrial revolution had transformed the cloth milling trade, leading to a boom in sheep farming and wool: a gentleman could make good money from farming his estates. A gentleman could augment his fortune by marrying the richly-dowered daughter of a lawyer, banker, tradesman, industrialist, textile mill-owner, or even, further afield, an owner of sugar plantations in the West Indies or one of those new Nabobs who had made fortunes from the spread of British influence in the East Indies; the gentleman could feel he was doing his wife a favour by giving her a leg up the social ladder at the same time. By the late 18th century, the Chadwick family's fortunes – boosted by advantageous marriages – included Lancashire cotton mills.

FOLLOWING PAGE: The Yew Walk, planted in the 1500's by the Sacheverells. Over 18 trees ensured a steady supply of yew for longbows, as well as an elegant, shady place to walk.

OPPOSITE: One of the many glorious stained glass windows installed by Charles Chadwick in the lower hall.

When young Charles inherited in 1793, his father, Colonel John, turned his passion for doing up country houses – with his wife's money – onto New Hall. Colonel John ordered extensive alternations to make it more picturesque. The windows were enlarged to allow the light to stream through. The bay on the west side was widened and a tower was built above it. Although Georgian taste was still heavily Neo-Classical, Gothic architecture was just starting to become fashionable again amongst a few brave souls: New Hall, genuinely ancient, would have been at the cutting edge of design.. The extensions were in brickwork with red stone quoins and Gothic windows, embellished with crenellations, as befitted New Hall's medieval origins. A carved stone on the tower bears the date 1796 and the initials IC, FC, CC, HMC and MC - that is, John Chadwick (Charles' father), Frances, (Charles' wife), Charles himself, Hugo Mavesyn Chadwick his son, and Mary Chadwick - Charles' sister who died young. Charles himself ordered some exquisite painted glass from Flanders, representing legendary figures, and placed these throughout the house, particularly in the bay windows of the Banqueting Hall. Charles also put together a valuable collection of books and paintings.

1800
Moving to Mavesyn Ridware as the Money Starts to Dry Up

Between 1797 and 1800, a plain Georgian house, known as Upper House but later called Ridware Hall, was also built on the Chadwick's other estate at Mavesyn Ridware. This was part of the inheritance from Aunt Dorothy, who died when her bonnet caught fire in 1784. Despite all the work Colonel John had done to New Hall, Mavesyn Ridware became Charles' principal seat, possibly because it was a smaller, more manageable house; moats and the ghosts of incestuous Satanists are not to everyone's taste. After a life of building and collecting, Charles began to run short of money and had to rein in his profligacy. By the end of his life – and he long outlived his wife, Frances - he was said to be very tightfisted. As Sarah Holbeche recorded in her Diary after a visit to New Hall: 'New Hall. Old, haunted and uninhabited except Isaac and Rebecca Grimley living in the great low kitchen and room over it, leaving the towers and turrets to the owls and bats..... '

1829
Hugo Mavesyn Chadwick, World Traveller

When Charles III died in 1829, New Hall and Ridware Hall were inherited by his son, Hugo Mavesyn Chadwick. Hugo is recorded as living at Ridware Hall in 1829, as his father had done before him, along with his wife, probably because of the increasingly dilapidated state of New Hall. To manage the debts, Charles had placed all his estates into a trust which allowed Hugo an income of around £2000 pounds a year - about £250,000 per annum today. Hugo's son, John Charles Healey Mavesyn Chadwick, was born in 1834, in Ridware Hall.Shortly afterwards Ridware Hall was rented out. New Hall itself was rented by a farmer, who used most of its vast rooms for storage. The world was beginning to open up to the well-heeled traveller for pleasure, and Hugo, houses in England rented out, took advantage of it. He spent the large part of the 1830's travelling to exotic locations but eventually came home for good. He settled in New Hall, which was still in the hands of the Trustees. Hugo spent a considerable amount of money restoring the house. Before Hugo Chadwick died in 1854, Callow estate was sold by the trustees to pay off debts. New Hall and Mavesyn Ridware were left to Hugo's son, John Charles Healey Mavesyn Chadwick. John Charles was only 20 when his father died.

1691

OPPOSITE: An example of 19th century Indian pottery sits on top of a remaining Chadwick carved Tudor chest, in the corridor leading to the moat garden.

1857
The Indian Mutiny and the Last of the Chadwicks

John Charles Chadwick of New Hall, like so many young gentlemen of his time, was a soldier, a Lieutenant in the Second Dragoon Guards, before transferring to the Queens 9th Lancers. The 19th century was the great age of the growth of the British Empire and once again New Hall and its occupants reflected what was by now British – rather than English - society. John Charles was to play a role in one of the defining episodes of 19th century British Imperial History, the Indian Mutiny (or First Indian War of Independence) of 1857. This was the greatest crisis to face the spread of British power since the American War of Independence in 1776. In May 1857, when the Uprising began, India, although in British hands, was run by a commercial organization, the Honourable East India Company. The East India Company – known as "John Company" - had been slowly increasing its holdings in India for nearly two hundred years, and now controlled most of the country through its own private army, run by British officers, using largely Indian troops. That year the Indian soldiers – known as Sepoys - in John Company's army - rose up against their officers and the British settlers. A wave of violence swept through the country, with British men, women and children being killed indiscriminately. The British Government hurriedly sent out reinforcements from Britain to restore order; John Charles's regiment was sent to Calcutta from England in November 1857. John Charles fought with distinction at the Relief of Lucknow. The capital of the recently-annexed princely state of Oudh, Lucknow was the scene of one of the longest and most brutal sieges of the war. The casualties included hundreds of women and children, holed up in the compound of the British Residency. They faced a force of estimated at between 30-60,000. The siege lasted from 30 May to 27 November 1857.

It is estimated that some 6000 British men, women and children were killed during the uprising, out of the 40,000 or so then living in India. In the reprisals, British troops were said to have killed many times that number – with some 150,000 killed in the state of Oudh alone. John Chadwick would have played some part in this. Officers at the time described how their men were "tired of killing" during the seemingly endless executions, as the British attempted to make sure such an uprising never threatened them again.

John also met his wife in India during his time serving there. The 1861 census documents the following occupants of New Hall "John Charles Chadwick, aged 26 and described as a landed proprietor of Bath and his wife Clara aged 20 who had been born in Agra in the East Indies". Clara was the daughter of a a Major Good, of the Bengali Cavalry. The census goes on to record that they had a one-year-old son and daughter who had been born the previous month. Staying at the house as visitors were John Charles Chadwick's cousin, Clara South, from Surrey, and his brother-in-law, Frederick Goad, an ensign of the 72nd Highlanders, who had also been born in the East Indies at Shimla.

Unfortunately, John Charles inherited his grandfather's extravagance. Once he had left the army and returned to New Hall with Clara, the couple led a colourful life and were said to throw enormous parties – New Hall throbbed with fun, as it had never done before. As well as being a Justice of the Peace and Deputy Lieutenant of the County of Warwick, John Charles was a keen horseman. He hunted with the South Staffordshire Hounds and supported the local steeplechases - the Birmingham Steeplechase was held at that time in Sutton Park. John was known to both own racehorses and be an enthusiastic gambler. He seemed to be spending his inheritance at an eye watering rate. In 1867 John Charles is recorded as having borrowed £5226 from Robert Landor of Rugeley - about £600,000 today - and shortly afterwards, he began to enlarge New Hall.

1868
Victorian Gothic

In 1868 John Charles began his extensive renovation of New Hall. John Charles was a man of his time, and the Victorians' attitude to country houses was the bigger and more ornate the better. New building techniques, developed through the industrial revolution, meant that architects and builders were able to experiment with extravagant ways to ornament new and existing buildings. Thanks to the Victorians' romanticization of all things Medieval, Gothic architecture was the very height of fashion and New Hall, the real deal, would have been a gem. And with the Victorians' magnificent self-confidence that the sun would never set on the British Empire, John Charles set out on his improvements with gusto.

He brought in renowned Birmingham architect Yeoville Thomason, who also built Birmingham's Council House - the seat of opulent Midlands' power. Thomason added a tower, a dome and installed a magnificent glass porch over the bridge on the moat. This included a picturesque roof supported on carved oak pillars. An extra storey was added to the main building, along with an array of new windows made from sandstone and mullion-transom windows along the western façade. The North wall was rebuilt to match the darker sandstone of the original house. Many other features were added, including emblazoned parapets, carved with the date of 1870.

1879
The Age of the Train

In 1879, the area around New Hall, like so much of the Britain, was transformed by the building of railways. The new Midland Railway Walsall Branch line was built, stopping at Sutton Coldfield. Inevitably, part of the railway line ran across New Hall's land, something which John Charles would have been compensated for. It's hard to over-estimate the transformation the railways made to people's lives, socially and economically. Instead of having to rely on slow carriages on pot-holed roads, riding horseback or walking - depending on what you could afford – travel became accessible, reliable, swift and cheap. Tourists started to come out to Sutton Coldfield for the day, to escape the smog and noise of Birmingham's booming industrial metropolis. The middle classes, who worked in Birmingham, could dream now of living further out, in the green countryside, instead of being tied to a house within walking distance of their desks.

1880
The Beginning of the End

Whatever John Charles was paid for the Railway line, it wasn't enough John Charles ran up considerable debts that he was unable to repay.Another loan, this time of £40,000 – about £5 million today - was taken out against his estates in 1880, in order to help settle some of his debts. In 1881 the Chadwick Sale was organised to sell off some of New Hall's assets, including the chandeliers from the Great Chamber. These were bought by a Mr Chatwin for his home in Edgbaston, a smart new leafy suburb near to Birmingham. Around this time, 1882, the Aston Rural Sanitary Authority laid main sewers to the Hall as part of an attempt to bring sanitation to the area,but that must have been little consolation to John Charles. The 1881 sale did not raise enough money and, by 1882, John Charles had been forced to move out of New Hall and was living in Brighton with his family.

RIGHT: New Hall as it was in 1850, showing the North East elevation; the wing on the left is the original Saxon ashlar keep, with Thomas Gibbons's Tudor North wing in red sandstone on the right.

BELOW RIGHT: Yeoville Thomason's architectural plan for the same elevation – realising the Gothic fantasia with additions of tower, dome, an extra storey and crenellations everywhere.

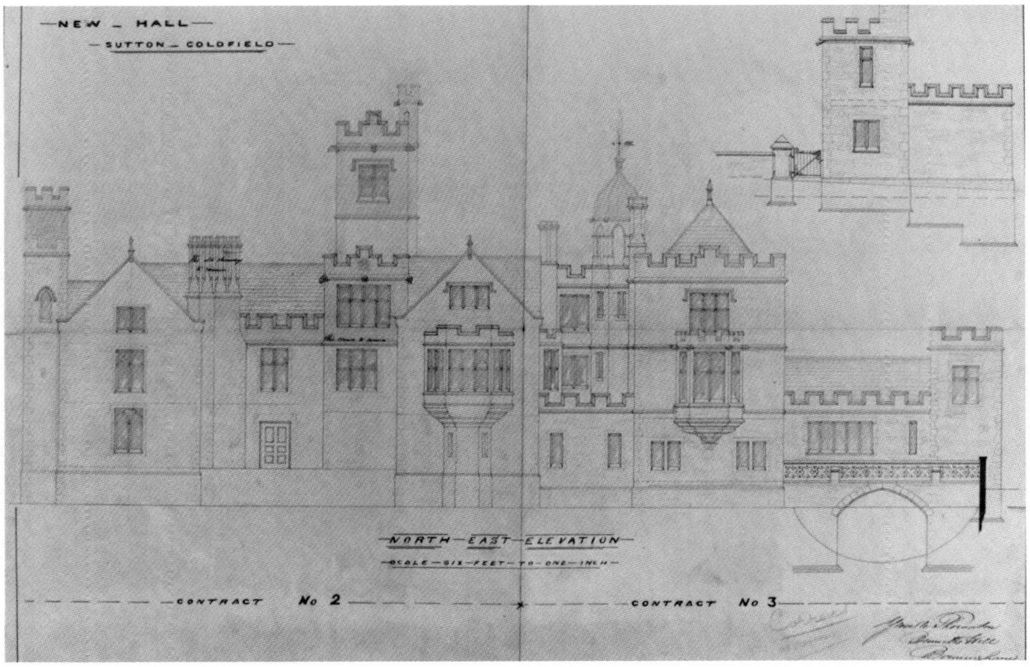

1883
The End of the Line

On, May 7th 1883, John Charles was declared bankrupt in a Sussex court. According to historian Mark Eades, "It took 800 years to accumulate a fine estate in Staffordshire, Warwickshire, Derbyshire and Lancashire and one profligate generation to lose the lot!" The ownership of the of New Hall passed to John Charles' mortgagees. New Hall was put on the market shortly afterwards - the house's days as the home of the landed gentry were over.

6.

THE BEST YEARS OF YOUR LIFE – NEW HALL GOES TO SCHOOL

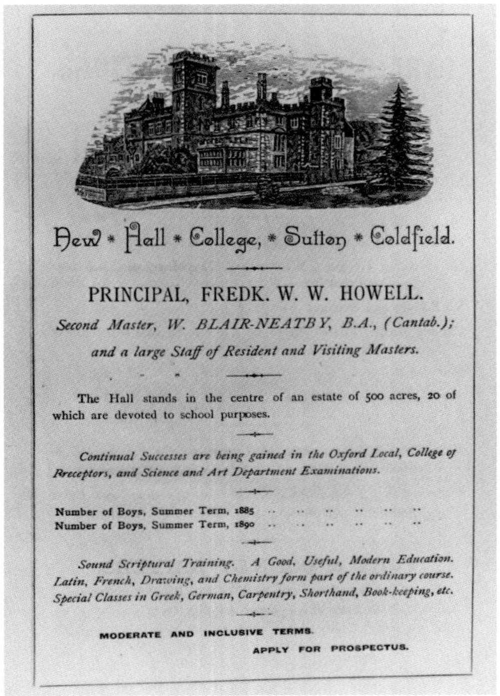

ABOVE: Advertisement for New Hall College Boy's School in the Sidwell and Durant Guide, 1890.

1885
New Hall College

New Hall's next incarnation was as a boys' boarding school. Private education was another late Victorian boom. With the advent of the railways, and the rise of the middle classes, more people wanted to educate their children formally, rather than with private tutors at home. Plus, with the spread of the empire, there were jobs available for young men who had been educated to cope with living far away. Following the model of the great public schools founded around the time of the Renaissance and Tudor periods, such as Winchester, Eton, Harrow, Rugby, Charterhouse, Westminster and Shrewsbury, numerous private and public schools were set up during these years. Many of these schools survive today, such as Marlborough, Wellington, Haileybury, and Cheltenham College. They followed the pattern of the great 19th century educational reformer Dr Thomas Arnold, the headmaster of Rugby School. Rugby – not far from New Hall - was in fact founded in 1567 but was transformed by Arnold into the archetypal Victorian public school. Once again, New Hall was mirroring the prevailing social trend.

New Hall College opened in 1885, with Mr F Howell as the first principal. Unfortunately, Mr Howell drowned on a visit to Iceland in 1891, and a Mr Everard Healey then became the headmaster, running the school along with his son. It is open to question whether these Healeys were connected to the Healey Chadwicks who had owned New Hall for over a century, but perhaps they liked to think they were. Interestingly, there is no record, in fact, of any sale going through at this time, so it is likely the school actually rented New Hall estate from the Trustees. An advert for the school read: 'Delicate and backward boys receive special attention. There is every accommodation for boarders. The bedrooms are large, lofty, well-lighted and thoroughly ventilated. The Diet is thoroughly wholesome and unlimited milk and butter is procured from the private dairy. 20 Acres of land give opportunities for football, cricket, tennis and abundant facilities for fishing are afforded by the moat and ponds.'

The school had places for up to seventy boys who intended to pursue "professional or commercial careers" – carefully aimed at the Birmingham professional classes - perhaps a useful contrast to the grander Public Schools, who were churning out officers and gentlemen to run the Empire. French and German were taught and boys are recorded as having done well in external examinations. The school also offered activities in the carpenter's shop, the gymnasium and chemistry lab as well as military drill and singing.

ABOVE: Three generations of Healey headmasters, standing on the road leading to Walmley, next to the stables and coach house. Taken in 1895 by the pioneering photographer, Benjamin Stone.

RIGHT: The drawbridge entrance to New Hall in 1892, now Victorianized with a glass roof and panels and deemed a safer option with sixty schoolboys in residence.

ABOVE: At the back of New Hall, one of the senior boys poses in the skiff which was the only way to cross the moat to the back lawns and Yew Walk. One senses an inkwell on the verge of being thrown from the open window.

OPPOSITE: The Great Chamber was arranged to receive visiting parents and prospective new pupils.

PREVIOUS PAGES: The huge cedar trees that dominate the long walk next to New Hall's old kitchen garden are over 800 years old.

Initially, New Hall College was a success. When the Healeys first took over, there was only fourteen boys boarding but the numbers increased to 62 by 1893. The school made the most of New Hall's large and elegant rooms. The Great Hall was used as a dining room and the Great Chamber on the first floor for special occasions, and as a formal reception room for receiving parents and official visitors. The second-floor rooms with their lofty ceilings became airy dormitories, and the more formal first floor rooms on were classrooms. The second bridge across the moat was also enclosed. The chapel, which had been used as a coach house when the Chadwicks lived there, was converted into a carpenters' workshop and later into the school gymnasium.

Playing fields were laid out on the land surrounding the Hall and its gardens and, in 1902, electricity was installed. The sewage works newly laid by the Aston Rural Sanitary Authority in 1881 was a great attraction for parents, in an age far more interested in hygiene than previously. The sewers, a relative luxury at the time, would have made sanitation standards at New Hall infinitely superior to many other comparable schools. There were schoolboy tales of a vast and wily pike which lived in the moat and absolutely refused to be caught, and an old owl who lived in the tower, which was used as a "bogey" to scare new boys. The boys also had a habit of throwing inkwells into the moat: literally hundreds of inkwells were discovered when, in the early 1900's, a new owner had the moat cleared.

By 1902, however, the school was in financial trouble and was forced to close. New Hall was once again to change hands.

7.

THE WILKINSONS AND THE GOLDEN AGE OF COMMERCE

ABOVE: Walter Wilkinson and his wife, Emily Adelaide, in the grounds of New Hall, 1906.

RIGHT: The Great Chamber was refurbished with the chandeliers, sold by the spendthrift John Charles Chadwick in 1881, but tracked down and restored by the Wilkinsons. These priceless works of art hang there to this day.

OPPOSITE: New Hall's southeastern aspect, taken from beyond the lake by Benjamin Stone in 1907.

1903
The New Rich, Millinery and Property Development

At the turn of the century, in 1903, New Hall and its estate was bought by a Lt Colonel Walter Wilkinson. Despite his military title – which is shown on his tombstone - Wilkinson was a familiar 19th century phenomenon – a wealthy merchant, manufacturer and property developer, surfing the wave of the Midlands' economic boom. Wilkinson had made a fortune and he wanted a distinguished gentleman's residence as befitted his wealth – and thanks to the railway, it was easy for him to go between New Hall and the source of his fortune, his work premises in Birmingham.

Born in Leeds in 1849, Walter Wilkinson and his two brothers, Howard and Harry, inherited their father's successful wholesale fabric and millinery business, Wilkinson and Riddell. In the 1880's, when Wilkinson was in his early 30's, he and his brothers also inherited a considerable sum of money from their uncle, John Wilkinson, a successful property developer. With this money, the brothers invested heavily in land and property around the swiftly expanding manufacturing metropolis of Birmingham, as the formerly rural working classes flocked to the city for jobs, and the middle classes moved out to the commuter belts and suburbs. Wilkinson and Riddell, catering for this burgeoning market, also went from strength to strength. By 1888, the family firm was the largest wholesale textile merchant in the Midlands. By 1902, Wilkinson and Riddell had over seven thousand customers. Its shares were listed on the stock exchange, becoming a public company. The three brothers all did exceptionally well financially from the sale. In 1903, with his share of the cash - or some of it - Walter Wilkinson bought New Hall.

Walter and his wife Emily Adelaide Meakin returned New Hall to its former splendour. They modernised and redecorated the house and moving in, in 1904. In 1910, the Wilkinsons managed to track down and buy back the chandeliers from the Great Chamber, sold by the spendthrift John Charles Chadwick in 1881. They were

delighted to be able to return the chandeliers to their original place. They replanted the gardens, which bloomed again with a glorious variety of flowers and shrubs. The Wilkinsons had no children of their own but were close to Walter's brothers' and sister's children, who often came to stay. In the 1911 census, two of their nieces, Margaret Wilkinson, and Doris Lawden, were recorded as residing permanently at New Hall. The favourite nephew, John Wilkinson, was being groomed to be the heir to New Hall. A new Wilkinson dynasty seemed secure.

1896
Royal Hotel, Sutton Coldfield

Walter Wilkinson may have had his eye on New Hall for a while. In 1896 he bought the former Royal Hotel in Sutton Coldfield, a magnificent statement of High Victorian neo-classical architecture, complete witha quasi-Byzantine clock tower. The Royal Hotel had first opened in 1865, and as Birmingham expanded during the 19th century, Sutton Coldfield became a popular railway destination for trippers trying to escape the smog of this industrial metropolis. But the hotel was not a success financially, and closed after 30 years. Walter initially wanted to turn it into a Sanatorium, but in 1901 he sold it to the Sutton Corporation for £9000 – about £1,100,000 today. The Royal Hotel was transformed into Sutton Coldfield's Town Hall and opened in 1906. This meant that Walter spent considerable time in Sutton Coldfield, and he could not have failed to have come across the distressed gothic beauty of New Hall.

ABOVE: A visit by the Vesey Club to New Hall in September 1908. All the pictures were taken by Benjamin Stone.

OPPOSITE ABOVE: A visit by the Birmingham Geological Society to New Hall, 1907.

OPPOSITE BELOW: The great man himself, Benjamin Stone in 1902, whose images stand true today as genuine works of art.

Early 20th Century Edwardian Splendour

The first decades of the 20th century were the apogee of Empire and Edwardian impervious self-confidence. Britain was still the richest country in the world. Although not movers in high society, the Wilkinsons were highly respected and powerful in the region and very visible in public life. New Hall as a result became a buzzing social hub. The Wilkinsons often held garden parties - frequently for charity - in New Hall's grounds, where guests could wander the Yew Walk or, shaded by the cedar trees, listen to talks on New Hall's history, sitting on chairs, in the cool of the Moat Garden. One of the speakers was Sir Benjamin Stone, the distinguished Birmingham MP, industrialist, and photographer. The Victorian version of a Renaissance man, Stone, like Bishop Vesey, in whose honour Stone founded the Vesey Club, was another of the remarkable figures – absolutely men of their time – to be associated with New Hall and Sutton Coldfield. Stone's talk was lavishly illustrated with his photographs taken of New Hall over the preceding years, as well as other places of interest around Sutton Coldfield and the Black Country.

1838–1914
Sir Benjamin Stone – High Victorian Renaissance man

Sir Benjamin Stone was a man of many parts. A Birmingham industrialist, son of a glass manufacturer, politician and Fellow of many notable societies, including the Society of Antiquaries and of the Geological Society. He was a member of Sutton Coldfield Council - becoming Sutton Coldfield's first mayor when the town was made a borough in 1886, until 1890. Knighted in 1892, in 1895 he became the member of Parliament for East Birmingham, retiring in 1909. He was also appointed High Steward of the Royal Town of Sutton Coldfield in 1902.

Like many Great Victorians, Stone had enormous energy and intellectual curiousity. An ardent photographer who travelled extensively in pursuit of his hobby, Stone left a collection of over 26,000 black and white photographs, now housed in the archive of the Birmingham Library as the Benjamin Stone Collection. Many are of historical places of interest around Birmingham and Sutton Coldfield, but Stone also travelled as far afield as Brazil, Japan, Spain and Norway. He made an invaluable record of the folk customs and traditions of the British Isles and wrote of his purpose as being "to portray for the benefit of future generations the manners and customs, the festivals and pageants, the historic places and places of our times."

Stone was also a photographic pioneer, one of the first photographers to switch from wet to dry plates, taking away the need to develop the plates 'on the spot' as soon as they had been exposed. As an early President of the Birmingham Photographic Society, Stone helped to establish the Warwickshire Photographic Survey, which aimed to record for future generations the country's architectural and historical heritage.

1914–18
New Hall and The First World War

In June 1914, the heir to the Austro-Hungarian Empire, Archduke Franz Ferdinand, was assassinated in Sarajevo by a young Bosnian Serb Nationalist, Gavrilo Princip. The repercussions of that shot echoed around the world. A month later, what became known as the Great War broke out, shattering the post-Edwardian imperial summer. Walter's brother, Harry Wilkinson, was a Colonel - Vice Chairman of the South Staffordshire Territorial Association. Like so many others all over Britain, Colonel Harry raised a battalion of young volunteer conscripts for his regiment. It is likely that Walter Wilkinson too, was a member of the South Staffordshire TA, as he is referred to as Lt Colonel Wilkinson on his gravestone. In the preparation for war, reports show that the soldiers of the new battalion trained in the grounds of New Hall, before they were sent off to France and the slaughterhouse of the trenches of World War One.

Like so many regiments, the South Staffordshire suffered enormous casualties during the war – 6357 men were killed. And amongst the dead was Walter Wilkinson's favourite nephew and heir designate, who died aged 23, on 5th May, 1917, fighting with the Welsh Regiment, and is buried in the Longuenesse Souvenir Cemetery at St Omer. New Hall was without an heir. After the war, Walter Wilkinson's health was waning. In 1922, he went into hospital and died of a heart attack, during an operation. He was 74. The entire New Hall estate, valued at £138,000 – about £8,500,000 today - passed to his wife, Emily, but she sadly also died the following year.

As generous in death as they were in life, the Wilkinsons made various bequests to local hospitals and institutions. As they had no children, their fortune was shared between their surviving nephews and nieces. And with the death of their chosen heir for the estate, New Hall was put on the market once more.

The impact of the Great War on families in Britain immense. It's estimated that 886,000 servicemen and women were killed. Almost everyone in Britain lost somebody they knew and loved, and the loss of an entire generation of young men was to shape Britain's economy and politics for years to come. The war also saw the demise of many British country houses, as so many sons were killed and family fortunes reduced by war and death duties. It's not surprising, then, that the next owners of New Hall, Alfred Owen and his family, were also heavily touched by the First World War.

George Owen Birch (b1895 – d1914)

George Owen Birch of the Welsh Regiment was reported missing in action on 14th September, 1914, during the first Battle of the Aisne, in World War 1. George was the son of George Thomas Birch, the Rector of St Mary's Bucknall, Stoke-on-Trent, Staffordshire, and Elizabeth Owen Birch. Elizabeth was the aunt of Alfred Owen, who was to buy New Hall a decade later. Elizabeth had insisted on keeping her Owen family name on marrying. George was Alfred Owen's first cousin and they had grown up together. Alfred kept a photograph of George as a baby in a frame in New Hall along with a photograph of him in uniform. It is thought that Alfred Owen paid for the building of the monument to George in St Mary's Church in Bucknell after the war.

ABOVE: The South Staffordshire regiment, 6th Battalion, 1914, into which many of the Staffordshire Territorials were deployed.

OPPOSITE: George Owen Birch in regimental dress, 3rd Battalion, Welsh Regiment, taken in 1913 and donated to the Imperial War Museum by his mother, Elizabeth Owen Birch.

8.

THE OWENS – PLANES, CARS, TRUCKS AND BUSES

ABOVE: Alfred Owen, photographed at the Rubery Owen office in the 1920. At the age of 31 he was the Proprietor of Rubery Owen, the Proprietor of H M Joel & Co, steel smelters of Sheffield, the Chairman of Wellman, Smith, Owen Ltd, and Chairman of Brooke Tool Manufacturers.

In 1923 New Hall was bought from the Wilkinsons by the industrial magnate Alfred Owen. He had made his fortune in the booming late 19th and 20th century field of engineering. Like the Wilkinsons, Owen was one of the new breed of businessmen who liked to invest their new found wealth in one of the stately homes which were being sold by the 'cash strapped' gentry.

Alfred Owen was a man of some genius. He had been born in 1869 in Wrexham, Wales, and trained as an engineer. In 1893, he moved to Darlaston, a swiftly industrializing town in the coalfields of Staffordshire, now part of the metropolitan sprawl of Birmingham. As well as coal, Darlaston had factories that made nuts and bolts, and country people flocked to the towns and factories for work, and the opportunities offered. It was at Darlaston, linked to Birmingham and thus the world by the Grand Junction Railway and the Birmingham Canal, that John Rubery had previously set up his structural engineering business. And it was here that Alfred and John went into partnership to found Rubery Owen. Together, the two men created an engineering empire that would lead the world in developing steel as a lighter metal than iron which could be used for buildings, road and rail bridges, cars and aeroplanes and in the early 1900s had built the first pressed steel car chassis for a new car built by Daimler. Rubery Owen's rise seemed unstoppable – and as Rubery Owen grew, so did prosperity for the people of Darlaston.

When Alfred Owen bought New Hall, he was one of most successful businessmen in the Midlands. When John Rubery retired in 1910, he sold his shares to A E Owen. By 1912, Rubery Owen had expanded into aviation, and by the late 1920s Rubery Owen was growing rapidly. Owning a house like New Hall – within an easy 17-mile drive to his factory in Darlaston – was the logical step for a man of Alfred Owen's stature. His wife, Florence, was a very talented amateur artist and New Hall's glorious gardens and architecture provided inspiration for her work. Her grandson, David Owen, still has in his childhood autograph book the flowers Florence painted him in 1946.

Alfred Owen wanted to return New Hall estate to the size and importance it had enjoyed under the Sacheverell, Chadwick and Gibbon families. Although the estate was still reasonably large, Alfred Owen – backed by the fortune of his burgeoning engineering empire - set about buying back as many of the properties which had originally formed part of it, principally New Hall Mill and New Hall farm at opposite ends of the estate.

Alfred Owen had inherited with New Hall many antlers and 'big game' paintings but he was no hunter and wanted to furnish the hall with something unique to the nineteenth and twentieth century. He was also a great collector of the arts and was particularly interested in the revolutionary techniques of English Colour Printing. He built up one of the first complete collections of the pioneer George Baxter's prints, whose elegant hues and historically significant images would, he felt, be perfectly suited New Hall. The greatest part of his collection was put into a vault, waiting to be framed. Unfortunately, Owen suddenly fell ill. He was operated on, and at first seemed to improve, then sadly, had a relapse. In December 1929, at the age of 60, Alfred Owen died. He was buried at Sutton Coldfield Cemetery. Florence was widowed, alone with her children,Alfred, Ernest and Jean at New Hall.

On their father's death, Alfred and Florence's two sons, Alfred George Beech (AGB) and Ernest William Beech (EWB), took control of Rubery Owen but their mother, Florence, continued to live at New Hall and run the estate. Florence always welcomed visitors and guests to the house. The Vesey Club and other local institutions continued to meet at New Hall regularly, and the Owen family estimate that thousands of guests must have passed over New Hall's drawbridge and through its ancient, studded doors, during those days. Just as previous New Hall Ladies of the Manor would have kept an eye

TOP: Alfred Owen married Florence Beech on 27th June 1900, and they moved into their first home in Bescot, Walsall. The Rubery Owen employees were treated to a day out in August to Codsall Woods, which included dinner held in a large tent to celebrate the event.

ABOVE: New Hall from the North side, in 1910, after the Owens began to landscape the garden.

on the welfare of those working on their farms and estate - and the poor in the backstreet hovels of Sutton Coldfield - Florence also kept very much in touch with the workers and their families of Rubery Owen. She would often visit the works at Darlaston – driven by her chauffeur, Thatcher, round the industrial suburbs of Birmingham, in a large and regal Lanchester with fingertip gear levers. Thatcher, who worked for Florence for many years, had both a sense of humour and of what was appropriate to his mistress. Once, when the Lanchester bearing Florence was approaching Darlaston, she asked: "What is that terrible smell?" Thatcher quickly replied, "It is the sea breezes off the canal, madam".

During the Second World War, The New Hall estate was bombed several times by the Germans – another disadvantage of being so close to the industrial heartland of Birmingham. The main house was spared, because the moat had been camouflaged with leaves and branches, but one bomb landed in a field near the main drive leaving a large crater, while an unexploded bomb landed in the spinney and had to be detonated. The Luftwaffe also tried to bomb the Rubery Owen plant in Darlaston, on 5th June 1941 – the company was making parts for military equipment and the British Army standard issue Brodie helmets. The German bombs missed the factory but fell instead on one of the nearby council estates, which had been newly built before the war. Eleven people were killed in the raid. One of the unforeseen consequences of both the air raids and – possibly – of Florence's generous Open House policy, was a burglary, shortly after the war. One night, a thief scaled one of the drainpipes, and climbed through a first-floor window. Until the war, that particular window had always been barred: the only window that wasn't directly above the moat, it was obviously the manor house's only weak point. During the bombing raids, the bars had been removed, in case the house was hit, and the family had to escape in a hurry. After the war, nobody had got around to replacing them. Florence was distraught over the loss of her jewels, many of which had enormous sentimental value.

In 1958, Florence Owen died in New Hall, the house she and Alfred had bought and loved, and where she had presided for so long. She was 88 years old and had lived in the house for 35 years.

ABOVE LEFT: Florence Owen on the south lawn, with Bingo. After Alfred Owen Senior died in 1930, she continued to live at New Hall until her death in 1958.

LEFT: The wedding of Alfred George Owen (AGBO) to Viva McMullan, October 1932, pictured outside the Tudor entrance to New Hall.

ABOVE: Grace Jenkins, nee Owen, in 1936 with Florence the gardener's daughter, walking towards the statue at the end of the Yew Tree Walk.

RIGHT: The Sutton Coldfield Preservation Society have tea on the lawn, after their inspection up on the roof (see Foreword), hosted by Florence, AGBO and Viva Owen.

1964–75
The age of AGBO and Viva – Sir Alfred George Beech Owen and Eileen Kathleen Genevieve McMullan

When Alfred Ernest Owen died, in 1929, his son, Alfred George Beech Owen – known as AGBO because of his initials – had to abandon the engineering degree he was studying at Emmanuel College, Cambridge, to take on running Rubery Owen, with his brother Ernest. It was a huge challenge for a twenty-one year old to take over that responsibility for the factory and its employees. Alfred was his father's son and showed tremendous energy, vision and competence.

Rubery Owen at that time was hugely successful. It had 1,600 employees, making it one of the largest family-owned business in Britain, and one of the leading manufacturing firms in the UK. Rubery Owen was by then making parts for cars,trucks,buses, aeroplanes and agricultural machinery.

In 1932, Alfred Owen married Eileen Kathleen Genevieve McMullan,nicknamed Viva. Florence wanted a new house to be built for them on the estate near to her. This was called The Highway and was built on farmland just off the main driveway to New Hall. For 32 years, it was to be the home for them and their five children, Grace, David, John, Jean and Jim. After Florence Owen died in 1958, New Hall stood empty again for the next six years, with the exception of a live-in caretaker. Alfred carried out extensive renovations, updating the kitchen, rewiring and replumbing the house. He finally moved into New Hall with his family in 1964.

ABOVE: The British Motor Racing Research Trust meets at New Hall, to discuss the P15 V16 concept model, a prototype it hoped would take on the world in Formula One racing. The Research Trust was established in 1947 to promote, finance and develop BRM. Sir Alfred is on the extreme left, with Raymond Mays, founder of the BRM, on the extreme right.

Like many owners of New Hall, Alfred Owen was a man of enormous energy and influence. As well as running Rubery Owen, Alfred took on many responsibilities in charities and education. He was a governor of Birmingham University, and became the first Pro-Chancellor of Keele University where Princess Margaret was the Chancellor. He became chairman of the Dr Barnardo's Children's Charity. He was an ardent supporter of the Boys Brigade, becoming a Vice President. They would often hold events and camps on land on the New Hall Estate.

Alfred was also asked to preach at many local churches and chapels, and was prominent in local affairs, firstly as a Councillor (1937–1974), then Mayor (1951) and Alderman of Sutton Coldfield. In 1954 he was awarded a CBE and in 1961 he was knighted Sir Alfred in the Queen's Birthday Honours list. In 1970 Alderman Sir Alfred Owen was made Freeman of the Borough of Sutton Coldfield - the last person to hold this office.

Just after the Second World War, Sir Bernard Scott, Chairman of Lucas Industries rang Alfred Owen to become a sponsor with him of Raymond Mays'project to build a British Grand Prix racing car. They were instrumental in establishing the first British Grand Prix Formula One racing car called BRM – British Racing Motors- with the help of many other sponsors from both companies and individuals. Unfortunately, the BRM project ran out of money and the sponsors agreed to support Alfred to take complete control in 1952. He formed a company as part of Rubery Owen called British Racing Motors Limited. In 1963, Sir Alfred Owen received the Ferodo trophy for the person who had contributed the most to British Motor Racing. Alfred managed BRM with the support of his sister, Jean and her husband Louis Stanley until 1969 when after Sir Alfred's stroke the role passed on to Jean and Louis Stanley to take complete control.

ABOVE: Sir Alfred and Lady Owen, shot by the greatest reportage photographer of them all, Henri Cartier Bresson, set against New Hall's backdrop of dreamy medievalism and splendid gardens in 1962.

ABOVE RIGHT: Cartier Bresson perfectly captured Sir Alfred as a man of purpose, energy and commitment, striding into the Rubery Owen offices each morning.

FOLLOWING PAGE: Another spectacular image shot by Cartier Bresson of Sir Alfred Owen in the Great Chamber, with his youngest son Jim Owen, 1962.

In September 1962, *Queen* magazine ran a profile of Sir Alfred, with the headline: "The Man who keeps the BRM on the circuits is also a Man of Charity". *Queen* produced an elegant quadruple page spread, lavishly illustrated with photographs, taken by the great reportage photographer Henri Cartier Bresson who also wrote the text and visited Sir Alfred at his home, The Highway. Cartier Bresson then accompanied Sir Alfred over several days as he went about his various engagements. *Queen* magazine described Sir Alfred as having: "That rare indefinable quality of goodness that makes him the devoted servant of those over whom, by birth and ability, he has been set." The photographs show Sir Alfred picking blackberries, singing hymns, walking on the lawn with his wife, and of his children having Sunday lunch with their mother.

Sir Alfred died on 29th October 1975. A service to commemorate Sir Alfred's life was held in St. Lawrence's Parish Church, Darlaston on December 5th, 1975, with an address given by David Sheppard,,the Bishop of Liverpool. Sir Alfred is buried in a new family tomb in Sutton Coldfield Cemetery. Viva, who died in 1995 was buried alongside him. An English Heritage Blue Plaque, honouring Sir Alfred's contribution to society, industry, and British Motor Racing, was installed at New Hall in 2005. Viva moved out of New Hall and back to the Highway after Sir Alfred's death and for six years, New Hall once again stood empty.

1975
Change is on the Way

After the death of Sir Alfred Owen at New Hall in 1975, Rubery Owen as the owners of New Hall were giving a lot of thought as to how best to maintain such a valuable asset. None of Sir Alfred's family wanted to live there as they were enjoying living in their existing houses. New Hall because of its size and the cost of the upkeep of the house and garden would have been something on which they would not wish to embark on. The UK economy at that time in the mid 1970s was really struggling with high interest rates, rising unemployment and inflation.

The vast forests of Sutton Chase surrounding this ancient hunting lodge had long vanished beneath the spreading mass of housing. The *Queen* 1962 piece describes New Hall and its park as being "An island of country surrounded by the industrial sea of Wolverhampton and Birmingham." A decade and a half later, the surrounding towns were creeping even closer. Rubery Owen as the owner of New Hall estate was looking at possible housing developments as a means of generating more income and therefore properties on the estate such as New Hall Farm, Warren House Farm and New Shipton Farm were seen as opportunities for development for housing.

Rubery Owen, like so many British engineering firms in the 1970s, were facing difficult trading conditions. Germany and Japan particularly were extending their exports as the UK was struggling with the increasing power of the trade unions.

As New Hall was owned as a company asset, the decision was taken in 1979 to look at the possibility of selling the house and gardens, along with its contents, to help stabilise Rubery Owen's finances. The Rubery Owen Group spent several years looking for a use for New Hall, including offering it to the National Trust. New Hall, with its moat, its sandstone battlements, cupolas and various gothic adornments, was always in need of considerable maintenance to keep it in good condition. One of the options was to talk to the National Trust as New Hall was a Grade 1 Listed Building. However,The National Trust wanted the Owen family to donate a considerable sum to endow the house and pay for the upkeep and running costs of its moat, two attractive walled-in gardens,and the trees and lawns of the extensive main garden. The family decided to keep the offer open while they looked for other possible opportunities for New Hall's future.

New Hall once again stood empty for several years. A previous employee became 'caretaker'and looked after the house and Mr Bill Irving looked after the gardens.

For the Twenty-Fifth Anniversary of the Queen's Coronation, a cricket match was held in the grounds for all the Owen family and other family and friends connected with New Hall. This was one of the last Owen family events to be held at New Hall and through local contacts it became known that New Hall and its gardens were up for sale.In 1981, a potential buyer was found.

1981
Goodbye to All That

In October 1981, the contents were put up for sale, separately, in a three-day auction in late October, organised between Phillips Auction House and the Midlands' firm of Edwards, Bigwood and Bewlay. The entire contents of the house were put into two large white marquees, erected in the turning circle in front of the main entrance. These sales

ABOVE: A statue of a lady covered in snow at the end of Yew Tree Walk.

ABOVE RIGHT: A young member of the family taking time off from the 1977 Silver Jubilee Cricket Match, the last private event hosted by the Owen family at New Hall.

marked the end of an era. The items sold reflect the lives of the inhabitants of New Hall over the centuries, the objects that were considered necessary or desirable for civilized life.

Lots included: "A Bluthner grand piano, a full-size snooker table, fine 18th and 19th Century oil paintings and family portraits, the penultimate part of the well-known Owen collection of Staffordshire Pottery, porcelain, metalware, arms and armour, a good library of books, 17th and 18th and 19th Century English, Oriental and Continental furniture, European and Oriental carpets and rugs, bronzes, glassware, maps, prints and watercolours, the Penryn Estate 19th Century Fire Engine, an early Ferguson tractor and agricultural implements, household and outside effects, plants etc." The sale attracted considerable attention, with a world record being set for the sale of a 19th Century American Sofa by J. H. Butler of New York, that sold for £21,000 to an American buyer, about £82,000 today.

1982
The Future

New Hall, its gardens and its immediate outbuildings were bought by Michael Blakemore, a businessman from the Midlands. In 1985 Blakemore sold New Hall to the Thistle Hotel Group. At present it is owned by Hand Picked Hotels.

9.

CHECKING IN AGAIN – NEW HALL HOTEL

1985
The Thistle Years – Pavarotti, Bon Jovi and Kylie Minogue

New Hall's beauty, unique atmosphere and spectacular history have turned it into one of the best loved hotels in the Midlands. In 1985, Thistle Hotels, seeing the house's bought New Hall and 26 acres of surrounding land. They undertook extensive restoration work on both the house and surrounding buildings. The renovations took nearly three years, and New Hall Hotel didn't open its doors to guests until 1988, under the management of Ian and Caroline Parks and the Thistle Hotel Group.

Realising the need for further bedrooms, The New Wing was built on the site of the old walled Kitchen Garden in 1992. The extension was designed by the architect Peter Inston, a specialist in renovating country houses of historical significance; his other work included renovating the spectacular Taymouth Castle hotel, former home of the Marquis of Breadalbane, on Loch Tay, in Perthshire. The New Wing, with its courtyard garden, sundial, mullioned windows and Tudor-style cupola, fits elegantly with the original house. The aim - to create more space without disturbing the fabric of the original moated Hall – seems beautifully achieved. In a hundred years, it may be hard to tell, as it was for Pevsner, where the one age of New Hall stops and the other begins. In 1995, a new spa was built in the grounds, housing a swimming pool, gym and treatment rooms. The walled rose garden was re-planted and the fishpond cleared.

Just as New Hall once hosted the luminaries of each age - Warwick the Kingmaker, Henry VIII, the fiery Dr Henry Sacheverell, and Formula One's Sir Alfred Owen – New Hall Hotel has hosted some of the princes of the modern Age of Celebrity. The late Luciano Pavarotti, world famous Italian tenor, often stayed at New Hall, when appearing in opera at the NEC in Birmingham. The hotel management is said to have spent £4000 creating a luxurious ground floor suite for the portly singer because, it was reported to the Birmingham Mail that Pavorotti found it too exhausting to climb the hotel stairs after a performance. The rock musician, Jon Bon Jovi apparently fell in love with New Hall: he filmed the video for his song "I'll Sleep When I'm Dead" in both the grounds and Great Chamber. His band turned up the bass so loudly that the moulded plaster work cracked with the vibrations.

The singers Robbie Williams and Kylie Minogue have also stayed at New Hall while performing in concerts in Birmingham - although it is believed they stayed in one of the nine feature rooms in the original hotel, now named after a variety of the water lilies found in the moat, rather than the suite created for Pavorotti.

The Great Chamber is now used primarily for private functions and weddings. The Bridge restaurant – serving a magnificent Sunday lunch - is in the oak-panelled room on the ground floor, formerly Florence Owen's morning room. The bar opens out onto the terrace and rose garden, surrounded on three sides by the moat, which continues to be fed by the seven underground springs.

2008
Hand-Picked Hotels

In 2008 New Hall was sold to the Hand-Picked Hotel chain and, in 2022, as this book was going to press, Hand-Picked Hotels are still running New Hall, a hundred years since the Owen family first bought it. And, just as the owners of New Hall provided jobs and a community hub for Sutton Coldfield for centuries, once again there are the same opportunities for those who live nearby.

RIGHT: The ancient greenhouses, which had provided bountiful produce for the house were situated in the old kitchen gardens, but had fallen into disuse and disrepair.

BELOW: The New Wing was built on the site of the old greenhouses, sensitively designed by the architect Peter Inston match the red sandstone and Tudor features of the original house. It provides a further 50 ensuite bedrooms.

PREVIOUS PAGE: A detail from the exclusive Princess Elizabeth suite, once the bedroom of Florence Owen, showing a Tudor chair rumoured to have been used by Henry VIII on a hunting visit to New Hall.

FOLLOWING PAGE: The Tudor Wall in what was once New Hall's private rose garden, now a romantic setting for wedding receptions, with an ingenious sheltered arbour for sitting.

FOLLOWING PAGES: The Topiary Garden, now part of the Terrace Lounge and Bar, where alfresco drinks and dining can be enjoyed. The topiary frames the mini arboretum behind, a remnant of the Owen's landscape designs of the early 1900's.

The Ghosts of New Hall

Given New Hall's age and the events the house has witnessed, it's unsurprising that over the centuries memories and lost dreams have left their mark on the house. Those who have lived and worked at New Hall have often said they feel that the house is haunted. New Hall Hotel has put together some research which lists the ghosts people say they have seen or felt.

A lady in white is said to haunt the Red Landing; no-one knows who she is supposed to be, but perhaps she is the wife of Henry Sacheverell, who died in the 17th century. Sacheverell abandoned his wife and left the hall to his illegitimate son, Valens, by his lover, "Mistress Keics".

A disembodied head is supposed to haunt the grounds of New Hall. As mentioned in Chapter Five, in the 18th century, the soldiers of the "Butcher" Duke of Cumberland, heading north in pursuit of Bonnie Prince Charlie, apparently executed and beheaded an unfortunate local man with a cleft palate: they allegedly thought he was a spy because they could not understand what he was saying. His disembodied skull can apparently be seen floating across the park, in search of his body. Less sensationally, a lady in dark clothes is sometimes seen walking a dog on the driveway, near the old kennels. Amongst others, she apparently was seen by the gardener's children, and held her hand out to them, as you might to a child.

Even today, in 2022, staff working at New Hall regularly report some eerie experiences, where ghosts are heard and felt but not seen. Incidents such as footsteps and unnatural chills, in the Great Chamber where the wretched George Sacheverell – according to legend, incestuously obsessed by his sister - scratched unrequited love poems in Latin on the mullioned windows, are regular occurrences. As George was also said locally to be an alchemist, in league with the devil, it's perhaps unsurprising that he has a restless spirit. Residents have recalled having heard a "loud crashing noise" in what is now the Oak Room, but was once the secret study where George Sacheverell practiced his alchemy.

Urgent voices and galloping horses can sometimes be heard after dark, in the circle at the end of the Yew Walk. And people have reported, in the rooms around the Great Chamber, hearing someone humming to themselves, as though they are at work, as well as foosteps in the narrow corridor leading to the Priest's Hole.

Staff on reception have told the authors of this book of recent sightings of a little boy, standing diagonally across from the check-in desk. As the receptionist stood up to see why this little boy was up so late (it was past midnight) he vanished. Yet in the middle of the flagstone floor were the imprints of tiny, wet feet leading away from reception which she was obliged to fetch a mop to wipe up. A few months later, a different staff member was manning the check-in desk. When she stood up, after her shift, to leave, the same set of tiny, wet footprints led away from the middle of reception, northwards into the wall. Neither receptionist had seen nor spoken to each other about this incident; both are adamant they had the same experience.

There are rumours that, during the time that New Hall was a school, one of the smaller boys drowned in the moat. What gives this tale a chilling credibility is that the reception area of the hotel is built over what used to be the pathway that ran along the bank of the north face of the moat.

PART TWO

THE ESTATE

1.

NEW SHIPTON FARM

ABOVE: As the population stabilized and increased, the market for grain expanded correspondingly. New Shipton Farm was no exception as its fields were increasingly turned over to the growing of wheat, oats and hay. Before mechanisation, the methods of ploughing and sowing the fields by hand remained the same for hundreds of years, and this picture taken in 1895, shows no change since 1600.

RIGHT: In 1895 the wheat was still harvested manually. It would be gathered into sheaves and the sheaves themselves were then brought together so that they could be leaned upright into each other to form a stook. This provided a temporary protection against adverse weather conditions before the wheat was gathered on to carts to be taken to New Hall Mill for threshing.

LEFT: Once the wheat was dried, it would have been transported to the New Hall Mill for threshing. The bundles or 'stooks' were laid on the mill floor and threshed with a 'flail', a long wooden pole with a chain and shorter wooden stick. This separated the wheat from the chaff, and stems which were turned into straw and used for livestock bedding.

BELOW: After the Midland Railway line was built across New Shipton's land in 1879, the fields beyond the railway remained with the farm. These fields ran beside the Plantsbrook stream (the same one that feeds New Hall Mill) and contained a number of osier beds, used for basket making. These fell into disuse as different materials started to replace reed baskets.

New Shipton Farm formed part of the vast Manor of Sutton Coldfield when it was held by the Earls of Warwick. The old Manor House of Sutton stood on Manor Hill, and its lands included a dairy farm and deer park. At some time in the 13th Century, the Earl of Warwick decided to re-organise his affairs at Sutton, building a new manor house with a moat at New Hall and establishing a new "Shippon" or dairy farm, that came to be called New Shipton.

The Earl's officials, led by the Receiver General – essentially, his Chief Executive - managed the estates to ensure that they were well run and profitable. Much of the land around Sutton was used for hunting but also, increasingly, for farming and the growing of wheat, oats and hay, with increasing amounts of land coming under cultivation.

Origin of the Word Shippen

Shippen – as in New Shipton - was first recorded in the Domesday Book as a farm called Scipene, meaning "cattle-shed". The name became common for referring to any building housing cattle. The name Shipton could also derive from sceap tun, "sheep farm" in Anglo-Saxon. The keeping of sheep was part of a mixed agricultural economy in the woodland and pasture area of the Midlands, which included keeping livestock as well as the growing of vegetables and cereals.

In 1401, Richard de Beauchamp, when he became Earl of Warwick, came to New Hall with his Receiver General, then a certain John Baysham, to review the rents and privileges of the inhabitants, and give new leases to his tenants.

In 1430, John Verney, a former Chaplain at Sutton Manor, was appointed Warwick's Receiver General; one of the perks Verney received was the tenancy of New Shipton Farm. This is one of the first records there are of New Shipton, for which Verney paid a rent of £4.12s.8d 12 shillings a year – about £4,600 today. The 160 acre farm gave Verney the status of a gentleman. Thanks to Warwick's patronage, Verney's career, by the time he died in 1457, included the prestigious posts of Dean of Lichfield and Archdeacon of Worcester.

In 1443 Robert Kelynge, the bailiff for Sutton, recorded all the income and expenditure for Richard de Beauchamp. One of these records cites "Manorial `income" which related to income obtained from property directly owned by the Lord of the Manor, with one of the farms recorded as "Le Newshippen"

At this time, New Shipton Farm was made up of four fields that were used for pasture, grouped to form a dairy farm. A large timber cruck framed barn was built to thresh the hay and house the cattle in winter. The barn, which still stands at New Shipton, is one of only seven cruck framed medieval buildings in Birmingham; like New Hall itself, it is likely that this barn was built to replace an earlier structure. The barn is built from five pairs of oak crucks and the oaks trees from which the crucks were made have been dendrochronologically dated to having been felled between 1424 and 1425. It is thought the barn was built in 1428 or 29 after the wood had been allowed to season.

The giant A frames support the room independently of the walls and are made from the two halves of a single oak tree, split down the middle. The farm's four fields were called Stoking, Grenestyfield, New Park and the Olderedyng. Stoking, means newly cleared land. Grenestyfield is a field where broom and gorse were hard to eradicate. New Park is a field next to a new deer park that had been made at Echelhurst. Olderedyng (which is now the car park at New Hall Mill) means anciently cleared woodland.

BELOW: Inspection of New Shipton Farm 'cruck' barn prior to restoration which began in 2005. The barn was built in 1428-9 from oak trees felled on the New Hall estate, and is one of only seven, rare, cruck-framed medieval buildings in Birmingham. As part of a prestige housing development, the barn is now home to an interior design firm.

The fields covered about 160 acres between the farmhouse and Penns Lane and are likely to have been bought into cultivation in the 13th century to meet the increasing demand for grain. As their names show, they would have previously formed part of the Demesne woodland that belonged to the Lord of the Manor.

As for John Verney, the tenant for life, Robert Kelynge recorded: "This being his 13th year, John Verney is to maintain all the buildings of the said Messuage and the fences for the said fields in all necessary things at his own expense except that the lord will supply structural timber for building repairs and underwood for the maintenance of said fences."

In 1480 a similar account documents that Richard Dey had taken over the tenancy in 1455 at an annual rent of £4.13s.8d – about £4,700 today - which was paid in 1480 by his widow, with King Edward IV being noted as the Lord of the Manor (this was shortly after Warwick the Kingmaker's estates were forfeited to the Crown after his death 1471 at the Battle of Barnet, in the Wars of the Roses). New Shipton remained in the ownership of the Lords of the Manor after 1528, when Sutton received its charter which made it a self-governing town.

LEFT: New Shipton Farm in 1979. By this time both the house and the barns were falling into disrepair. Rubery Owen Holdings carried out a survey to see what could be done, but no action was taken and the buildings continued to deteriorate until they became uninhabitable.

BELOW: The exterior of New Shipton's Grade II listed, medieval cruck barn, as it was during the Rubery Owen review.

RIGHT: The Walmley Local Action Plan of 1990 was created to manage the population explosion which had seen a small village of 1300 inhabitants increase to over 17000. The plan aimed to redevelop, as sensitively as possible, any derelict, local buildings of interest.

BELOW: The architectural plans for the barn, converted into offices that ran alongside the restored farmhouse, right. The site is now known as Country Park View.

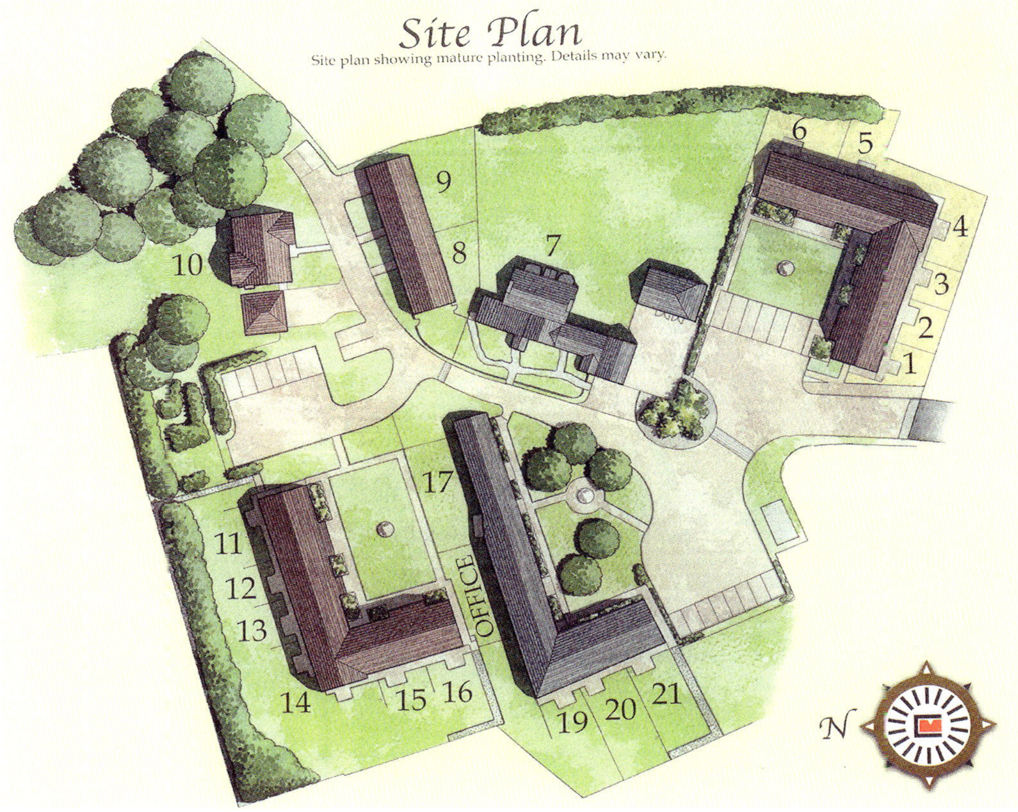

Artist's impression of New Shipton Farm barn conversion showing mature planting. Details may vary.

Artist's impression of New Shipton Farm new build cottages plots 1-6 showing mature planting. Details may vary.

PREVIOUS PAGES: New Shipton Barns today, converted into comfortable offices, but retaining all the integrity of the cruck beam structure inside, and renamed Country Park View.

1500's

In 1547 the Corporation of Sutton (acting as the Lord of the Manor of Sutton) leased New Shipton Farm to Humphrey Fisher for 80 years at an annual fee of £4.6s.8d – around £5,000 today. At some point Humphrey Fisher's payment seems to have been treated as a Chief Rent since his descendants were still paying it even though they had become the owners.

1600's

As the 16th Century stabilized, and the population increased, the market for grain expanded correspondingly. As a result, the farm is likely to have become a mixed farm, with the four fields being sub-divided to allow for both grazing and the cultivation of grain. A mill was built on the former New Park Field by John Penn, which became known as Penns Mill to support this increase in grain production. In 1617, a William Fisher is recorded as having sold Penns Mill, with about 40 acres of fields, to Robert Shilton of Birmingham.

Sometime in the 17th Century, the farm became part of the New Hall Estate, which by then Henry Sacheverell had purchased in 1610 for his natural son Valens. There is a record of George Sacheverell of New Hall mortgaging New Shipton Farm in 1673 to a London merchant called Thomas Falgate for £1000 plus interest – about £220,000 today. George Sacheverell – reliable in his unreliability - failed to repay the mortgage, and the farm passed to Henry and Humphrey Greswold. The Greswolds, however, claimed to have better use for their money so they sold the mortgage to Humphrey Jennens and Robert Dodds. It isn't clear if any of these owners farmed it or acted as agents for tenant farmers.

1700's

George Sacheverell must have managed at some point to repay the mortgage because in his will he bequeathed "his Antient Messuage or Farmhouse called New Shipton and all the Barnes buildings lands closes leasowes meadowes and pastures...now in the occupation of John Dawson" to his niece Katherine Floyer, wife of Ralph Floyer of Hints and it then passed to her eldest son, Sacheverell Floyer. In the rental book of 1787 and 1788 Floyer is shown as paying one of the highest Chief rents in the Parish for the farm. The rent was higher than New Hall's, Moor Hall and Langley Hall combined.

During the period of Floyer ownership, in around 1750, the medieval timber framed farmhouse was replaced by the brick farmhouse that still stands. It is situated on high ground, in the far north eastern corner of the property, facing what was for centuries the open commons. William Twamley was the tenant at the end of the 18th century and, in addition to the 120 acres, he also held the lease of New Hall Mill, with 30 acres of meadow and a rabbit warren. At the time the farm was leased from the Floyers of Hints Hall and the Mill was rented from Charles Chadwick, who then owned New Hall.

Twamley was obviously fairly well off and carried out extensive renovation work. He added some small rooms and bedrooms to the eastern side and a large kitchen and brew house to the south. At right angles to this extension, a small square two-storey structure was built, which housed ovens on the ground floor and a granary above. According to records held at Lichfield Joint Record Office, Twamley also purchased the tenancy of the property for 500 years for £2,500 – about £230,000 today - in order to protect his investment. The granary was accessed by an external ladder and would have been used to dry grain for grinding at New Hall Mill.

1800's

Until 1825 the farmer at New Shipton enjoyed common grazing rights on the extensive common lands of Sutton. The farmyard opened directly onto an expanse of common land known as New Shipton Field. Every Sutton farmer kept a flock of sheep which would graze freely on the commons. After 1825, the commons were enclosed, divided into fields and shared amongst those proprietors in Sutton who were deemed to be entitled. As a result, about 25 acres of land was added to New Shipton farm. These additional fields were located in an area bounded by the, then, newly set out Walmley Road and Wylde Green Common Road; access to the farm had previously been by unmarked tracks across the Common.

The first detailed plans of the farm date from the 19th Century; the schedule to the Parochial Valuation of 1856 shows that about half the fields were arable, with some low-lying fields meadow and the rest grazing pasture. Some leases for the other land in Sutton show that it was common practice to plough up a pasture field and put in crops of wheat, turnips, and barley in successive years, adding manure and lime, and then to sow grass and clover to return it to pasture. This rotation of crops - pretty much used universally before the advent of modern fertilizers - allowed the soil to regenerate.

In 1855, New Shipton was acquired by Baron Dickinson Webster of neighbouring Penns Hall – a JP, wire manufacturer and one of the pioneers of the underwater Atlantic telegraph cable. The Penns Hall estate had grown from the original Penns Mill and land from New Shipton. But Webster died suddenly in 1860 and his business partner, James Horsfall, took it over. John Ray was the tenant in 1851 with a household of ten according to the census. Joseph Todd took the farm over in 1856. He was still there in 1871, with three of his grown-up children and three servants. The Midland Railway line was built across the farm in 1879 but the fields beyond the railway remained with the farm. Beside the Ebrook (now called Plantsbrook) were some osier beds used for basket making. These fell into disuse as different materials started to replace reed baskets. Until recently, bomb craters from WW2 could still be seen in some of the fields.

1900's

When the Penns estate was sold in 1948, the farm and its land were bought by Sir Alfred Owen, who wanted to see the land returned to the New Hall Estate, 233 years after it had been sold. Rubery Owen Holdings took over the ownership of New Shipton after Sir Alfred's death and they continued to be let out to a farmer.

1979

By 1979 the farm was falling into disrepair. Rubery Owen Holdings carried out a survey to see what needed to be done to keep them in working order. No action was taken on New Shipton however, and the farm continued to deteriorate until the farm became uninhabitable.

2005

The Walmley Action Plan in 2005 called for ideas for redevelopment of the site. The old farm site was renovated. The barn was converted into offices, and the farmhouse and outbuildings into a variety of dwellings. The site, now known as "Country Park View", has preserved the cruck shank barn and surrounding buildings for future generations.

2.

BISHOP VESEY'S HOUSES

1520–40
The Bishop Builder

Bishop John Vesey remembered Sutton Coldfield of his childhood as a prosperous place. It had thrived under the patronage of first the Beauchamp Earls of Warwick. But its economy deteriorated sharply after the death of the the Kingmaker Earl of Warwick in 1471, as fewer people of importance now passed through the town, and its industry and farming had collapsed.

Vesey was very depressed when he returned and saw this decline. Being rich and generous, he invested heavily in the local economy and attempted to revive the wool trade to bring in new business.

Vesey was also an early pioneer of building good quality houses for workers in the community. He built a total of 51 stone houses in Sutton Coldfield, between 1520 and 1540, which aimed to provide secure and comfortable accommodation for workers. The houses were of similar type and style, and all were roughly based on a simpler design of his childhood home, Old Moor Hall, where he had returned to live.

The stone houses had quoins at the corners and timber frames inside. Doors and windows were framed by dressed stone. Interior walls used the latest building techniques of the time, made of oak beams filled with wattle and daub. Upper floors had wooden planks. Every house had a stone spiral staircase, a feature thought to have been inspired by the stone staircase at Moor Hall Farm where Vesey grew up.

Ford Keeper's Cottage

OPPOSITE ABOVE: Ford Keeper's cottage photographed in 1892, when the ford keeper would have been living there.

OPPOSITE BELOW: Ford Keeper's cottage photographed in 1988, fully restored and extended at the side.

One of the few surviving houses built by the Bishop, Ford Keeper's Cottage, is a small red sandstone building, now on Wylde Green Road. It is a typical example of the houses built by Vesey. The last remaining house with the original stone mullioned windows intact, Ford Keeper's Cottage stands next to where the old ford would have been used to cross the Ebrook (now Plantsbrook). This later became known as Wylde Green Road.

The ford keeper lived in what was known as the "Stone House" with his family. His job was to collect tolls from anyone who needed to cross the river. The tolls were paid to the local landlord. At the time, there was a wide marshy valley connecting Walmley to Sutton Coldfield, and the ford, where the river had been canalised, was the only place to cross safely. It was a very wide roadway, known as "Schemeford". The direction of the stream was altered when a new bridge was built on Wylde Green Road to carry the increasing amount of traffic, and the stream was then renamed Plantsbrook.

The interior of Ford Keeper's Cottage follows the typical design of all the Vesey Houses, although this was one of his smallest houses he built. It is just 30 foot long by 18 foot six inches wide. The original plan for the downstairs shows three rooms on the ground floor, a parlour, a larder, and a store. There were two bedrooms on the first floor and two more rooms in the attic, but only one with a window. The parlour had a fireplace, and in a piece of design that would still be seen as modern today, the flue ran up the outside of the house and also served a fireplace in the main bedroom upstairs.

For the working families, these houses, solidly built of stone, wood and brick, were a huge improvement on what they would have been used to. Bishop Vesey's determination to offer his community an alternative to the hovels they had lived in before was one of his lasting legacies. Today, Ford Keeper's Cottage has been modernised and extended, but the original parts and dimension can still be seen. It formed part of the New Hall Estate until it was sold in 1990.

LEFT AND BELOW: Warren House Farm pictured in 1978 prior to restoration and then in 2000, now a luxury home hemmed in by a modern housing estate. Its origins as a Vesey house are difficult to discern.

Warren House Farm

Hidden behind the houses off Walmley Road, is Warren House farm, one of Bishop Vesey's original 51 cottages. Built in around 1530, its distinctive stone spiral staircase, massive beams and projecting chimney are typical of Bishop Vesey's stone houses; although at 33 feet 6 inches long (10¼ metres), Warren House Farm is larger than the other houses.

There is a granary attached to the original cottage structure, which could predate the cottage, and a new a brick wing was added in 1671.

An early map of Sutton Coldfield shows the property as a working Mill – which seems likely considering its proximity to the Ebrook. (Plantsbrook). Built originally of stone, Warren House has now been covered in white stucco.

The house was built near New Hall on the far side of a forty-acre field that had recently been enclosed from Common land. It stands at the end of a long thin rabbit warren (conygree) which extended as far as Reddicap Hill, hence its name, Warren House. The field and the warren both belonged to New Hall, and Warren House itself was soon added to the New Hall estate. In the New Hall deeds of 1595, a "Conygree of 12 acres" is associated with New Hall which is lalmost certainly the same warren

The farmland belonging to New Hall was run from the home farm, which stood next door to New Hall itself for centuries. As extra land was purchased or reclaimed from the wild, it was added to Warren House Farm. Several barns were constructed which were used for animals, hay and grain storage.

Before the Enclosures Act in 1825, Joseph Hill of Warren House had a farm of 120 acres, while Isaac Grimley farmed 76 acres; Grimley's fields were in the centre of the estate, while Hill's were all round the edge, some as far away as Reddicap Hill.

At the time the whole New Hall Estate was owned by the Chadwicks. As part of the Enclosures Act Warren House Farm was awarded a further 20 acres.

By the 1860s William Dutton is recorded as being the tenant of both Warren House Farm and New Hall Mill, along with his daughter Ann. She married Henry Brockus and they lived at the Mill until his death in 1856, followed shortly afterwards by her father. The farm and mill then passed to Joseph and Thomas Dutton, possibly Ann's brothers.

In 1882, when the Chadwicks sold New Hall, the Sales Catalogue lists two farms, Warren House Farm, which now covered 142 acres, the Blabbs, New Hall Mill and Ford Keeper's Cottage; the area being used "for meadow, pasture arable, plantations and finely timbered land"

When Walter Wilkinson purchased the New Hall Estate in 1903, he moved the original farmyard from beside New Hall itself to a new site away from the main house, to what was called New Hall Farm (see below). At the same time, he re-allocated the farmland, so that Warren House had the southern half of the farmland, and the northern half pertained to New Hall Farm. The 1911 Census records Arthur Sweetman, a herdsman, living at Warren House, with his wife Eliza and daughter Annie, a laundry maid. William Kilburn, a farm waggoner and his wife, were also recorded living there, having moved from New Shipton where they were recorded living in 1901.

Farming at Warren House came to an end in 1990, when part of the land was given to New Hall Valley Country Park. Housing development took the rest, and, in 1998, Warren House and its barns were sold for redevelopment.

New Hall Farm

New Hall Farm was one of originally two farms that serviced the New Hall Estate, the other being Warren House. New Shipton also formed part of the Estate when it was first created; it was sold to the Penns Estate in the 18th Century but bought back in 1947 by Sir Alfred Owen.

The farms and land were made up of pasture for beef and dairy cattle, poultry and arable farming, which included potatoes, beetroot, barley, carrots, parsnips and oats. The produce would have been used to feed the estate workers and inhabitants of New Hall, with the grain produced being milled at New Hall Mill and baked into loaves.

Ordnance Survey maps of 1889, 1904, and 1920 show a well-established system of fields with the Ebrook (Plantsbrook) running through the base of the Valley, passing by New Hall Mill. The construction of the Midland Railway Walsall Branch, which was opened in 1879, changed the nature of some of the field boundaries but little else seems to change between the maps.

When Walter Wilkinson bought New Hall in 1903, he made some enormous changes. Wilkinson was obviously a great strategic thinker as a businessman and with regards to New Hall, he set about making some of the biggest changes yet to the estate. Wilkinson had New Hall's medieval farmyard – with its accompanying agricultural smells and noises - moved away from the main house, to a new site – known as New Hall Farm - at the edge of the estate. By the late Victorian and Edwardian eras there was an increasing understanding of the importance of hygiene. And, with Britain's internal stability it obviously seemed absurdly unlikely that New Hall might ever be besieged again, and, with improvements in transport, it was no longer necessary to keep food supplies so close at hand; equally, the advent of the motor car meant that you didn't need to have your horse stabled at your door. Instead of being reached from the main driveway, New Hall Farm was now accessed from Coleshill Road at the bottom of Reddicap Hill. The previous proximity of New Hall Farm to the Hall itself can be clearly seen in the ordnance survey map of 1899.

Wilkinson also re-allocated the remaining farmland, as mentioned above. The northern half of the estate now pertained to New Hall Farm, and Warren House had the southern half. In Ordnance Survey Maps of 1904 and 1920, a well-established system of fields, with the Ebrook (or Plantsbrook as it is now known) running at the base of the valley, shows little change from the 1857 field sizes and hedge boundaries; with the exception, of course, of the land around the Midland Railway Walsall Branch, which had opened in 1879.

In 1982, when the Rubery Owen Group sold New Hall Estate to Michael Blakemore, a lot of the land was sold off to property developers. New Hall Farm itself was demolished in 1984 to make way for a housing development, which is now called New Hall Farm Close.

Wincelle House

Moving Wincelle House was another of the improvement of New Hall's owner in the early 20th century, Walter Wilkinson: he had this ancient house taken down, transported three miles and rebuilt in New Hall park.

Wincelle House dates from the 15th Century. The wooden frame and other natural building materials were typical of building construction of the late medieval period. The name Wincelle came from "Winchicelle", the name recorded for the area named in the Domesday Book where the house was first built. Today known as Wiggins Hill, it is on the far side of Walmley.

RIGHT: Wincelle House, after its removal and reassembly, photographed in 2011.

FOLLOWING PAGE: The lane which leads from New Hall down to New Hall Farm, photographed by David Owen.

In 1432, the original Wincelle House is recorded, along with two others, as being held by a John Hore of Wishaw and Langley. It is in "circa 1559", that the house joins the New Hall estate, recorded as being sold by Robert Pudsey of Langley, Mayor (Warden) of Sutton Coldfield, to Thomas Gibbons of New Hall. 350 years later, in 1910, Walter Wilkinson had Wincelle moved from its original location. Instead, it was rebuilt closer to New Hall and New Hall Mill. To move the entire building safely the in-fill of "wattle and daub" of the wooden frame had to be taken out before the wooden struts of the structure. Every detail was meticulously recorded so that it could be rebuilt to its original design.

It was photographed at this stage of disassembly by the distinguished photographic pioneer, Sir Benjamin Stone, the MP for Birmingham East, and friend of Walter Wilkinson. A series of his images show a large timber framed building, with small square panels which probably date from the late 16th century. The timbers were next to be then dismantled and incorporated into the new house by the architects Marston and Marston who oversaw the project. This stage is recorded in their drawings. The infill was then replaced by more modern brick "noggin" and the interior was modernised. An extension was also built to the rear on the right to improve the domestic facilities.

The local Authority of Sutton Coldfield certified the new foundations as "satisfactory" in August 1910. The first occupant is recorded as being a Mr Benjamin Lorrimer in the electoral register of 1912–1913. It is rumoured that Mrs Benjamin Lorimer was a close friend of Mrs Wilkinson's. The two women wanted to live close to each other, so they could easily walk between each other's properties.

Wincelle was later sold to Alfred Owen in 1923 with the rest of New Hall estate. It stayed in the Owen family until 1980, when Wincelle was sold on the open market. A house called Elmhurst now stands on the original site at Wiggins Hill. It was built in 1922 and covers the exact footprint of where the original site of Wincelle once stood.
Wincelle is now Grade II listed and a private family home.

3.

NEW HALL MILL

New Hall Mill

New Hall Mill is still a working water mill for milling grain. It sits on the banks of the Plantsbrook, deep in the woods of New Hall park. Just six miles from the centre of Birmingham, New Hall Mill was one of thirteen water mills in the area, and of those thirteen water mills in Sutton Coldfield, New Hall Mill is the last survivor.

C16th
Thomas Gibbons

Parts of the Mill are thought to go back to the 16th Century, built on the instructions of Thomas Gibbons, who then owned New Hall Estate. Until the production of flour was industrialized, large estates to have private mills to make flour from grain grown on their farms. New Hall Mill, a charming building of local red brick with a tiled roof, was initially only one storey high, and the water wheel was originally driven by the water from Plantsbrook.

C17th
The Sacheverells

The first known reference to New Hall Mill was in 1610: the “New Hall Mills” were included in the sale particulars of New Hall's Estate, when the Gibbons to the Sacheverell family. Henry Sacheverell is documented as leasing the Mill out to various millers, during his tenure of the New Hall Estate. From milling corn for the New Hall Estate, the Mill, grew into a sizeable local business in its own right: in 1709 the Mill is known to have been leased to two Birmingham bakers. In 1710, George Sacheverell built another two and half floors onto the Mill, and added a house on the side for the miller to live in. When George, the last of the Sacheverells, died without an heir, the Mill passed with New Hall estate to his great-nephew, Charles Chadwick I.

ABOVE: A view across the banks of the Plantsbrook, the stream that fed the New Hall Mill waterwheels, 1901.

OPPOSITE: New Hall Mill in the late 1890's.

C18th and C19th – The Chadwicks

When the Chadwicks owned New Hall, a family called Dutton were documented as being the millers in the mid-18th century, with two working water wheels being in use. At some point, the Mill House became derelict and the miller, then recorded as being one Samuel Twamley, rented the nearby New Shipton Farm to live in. William Twamley, a miller and descendent of Samuel, is recorded as living in New Shipton Farm until the 1830's. William was renowned locally for campaigning for elementary education to be offered to all children living in Sutton. The 1861 Census records Joseph Brighton, 51, working as a miller and living at Mill House, so it seems by this point the property had undergone some form of restoration and was habitable again. The present mill machinery was installed in 1861, along with another set of machinery, which was put in at the North End of the Mill and was worked by the second water wheel. The alterations made to accommodate this machinery are clearly visible. The water wheels used were overshot – which meant the wheel was vertically mounted and rotated when water entered buckets which had just passed the top of the wheel. The wheel was made for a man called Thomas Price, a millwright from West Bromwich, by George Turton who had a brass foundry in Kidderminster. The water wheel measures eleven feet by six feet and has thirty-six buckets. The millstones, of which there were four at the time, and two remain, are French burrs and were installed by the same Thomas Price, the West Bromwich millwright. In the corner of the wheelhouse, by the shaft, a fireplace was built – the remains of which can be seen today. It is thought that, when the weather got very cold, the millers would light fires to prevent the water wheels from freezing up.

ABOVE: The millstones in 1940, prior to restoration. Millstones are the flat, round stones used to grind the grain.

OPPOSITE: The millstones in 1992, fully restored to working order.

PREVIOUS PAGE: The miller, Benjamin Styles, by the meal trough on the machine floor of New Hall Mill, 1902.

The second set of machinery and wheels were removed just before a new incumbent, Benjamin Styles, moved to the Mill in 1896. Styles, who came from Warwickshire, was to spend his life campaigning to save traditional mills like New Hall. For, by the 1880's, when the Chadwicks sold New Hall Estate and its mill, large steam mills were being built in towns and ports. Roller mills had been introduced in the 1870's and these were much more efficient than grinding grain with traditional mill stones. Small, traditional mills, like New Hall Mill, were finding it increasingly hard to compete.

In 1896, when Benjamin Styles came to live in New Hall Mill, the Mill had a new lease of life. Styles was someone who would be recognisable today - a pioneer in the campaign for the survival of stone ground whole meal flour, produced at mills like his. He was fighting against the new chemically-enhanced white flour which was now being produced in vast quantities by the new, industrialised, roller mills. By this time, the mill had reduced its operations to only one waterwheel, but that didn't daunt Styles. The following year, Styles is recorded as co-operating with a local baker and farmer to produce eighty loaves of bread from wheat which had been cut, threshed, milled and the resulting flour baked into loaves of bread - all in one day. Two of these loaves were sent to Queen Victoria as a gift for her Diamond Jubilee, in 1897: as a result, Styles gained a lot of publicity for the mill.

This feat, of milling and baking large numbers of loaves of bread in a day, has been repeated twice to commemorate the Silver and Golden Jubilees of Queen Elizabeth II in 1977 and 2002. Styles immortalised this act by having a poem written about it called "A Mill's Tale", playing on the name of "The Miller's Tale", Geoffrey Chaucer's famous 14th century poem about sexual shenanigans in medieval Oxford (although Styles's poem does noticeably lack Chaucer's genius, it has its own charm!)

Styles was also very keen on promoting his stone ground whole meal flour campaign in the local press, such as the Sutton Coldfield and Erlington News. His poem, "A Mill's Tale", and the gift to Queen Victoria formed part of this campaign.

Early 1900's
Wilkinsons

After Walter Wilkinson bought the estate, their friend, the distinguished 19th century photographer and Conservative MP for Birmingham East, Sir Benjamin Stone, photographed the Mill at around this time, adding to its fame.

In the 1901 and 1911 census, Benjamin Styles is recorded as living with his wife, Grace Emily Styles, at Holly Village, on Holland Road Sutton Coldfield. His occupation is given as miller. The 1901 census also records William Beccles as living at New Hall Mill, with his wife Bertha; his occupation is recorded as Batch Corn Miller, and he was employed by B Styles.

1923
The Owens

In 1923, when the New Hall Estate was sold to Alfred Ernest Owen, after Walter Wilkinson's death, Styles bought the Mill. However, he must have had second thoughts, for five years later, in 1928, Styles sold the Mill back to the Owen family. Alfred Ernest Owen was then buying back a lot of the land and assets that had formed part of the original New Hall Estate, including the land that formed New Hall Valley and New Hall Mill, and it suited him to bring the Mill back in hand. Styles' son-in-law, Charles G Davis, succeeded Styles as miller in 1929, followed by Styles' grandson, Ben Davis, shortly after World War 2.

David Owen, the eldest son of Sir Alfred Owen, remembers visiting the Mill in the 1940s and meeting Charles Davis when he was running the Mill. "He was always welcoming. He was tall and angular with sharp features. His clothes were covered with flour and he wore boots and buckled leather breeches. Once his aggressive cockerel chased me out of the yard back down the drive. Sometimes, in the summer, he told me 'the Mill's not running today because I have no water'".

ABOVE: The granary attic, used to store sacks of flour, photographed in 1952 in a state of decay.

OPPOSITE: The same granary attic, fully restored by 2001 and redesigned as a visitor attraction by the Friends of New Hall Mill.

The problem of a reduced water supply persisted during the tenure of Ben Davis, Style's grandson. It became increasingly difficult for Davis to maintain the flow of water needed to the power the mill wheel. In 1949, therefore, Davis installed a Ruston Hornsby diesel engine to power the mill, which was fitted into the opposite end of the mill to the wheel. The new engine meant Davis could continue to mill grain without having to rely on the water supply. The mill could be connected to a hammer mill, two combined milling machines, and could also work a sack hoist. This hoist still works to this day, powered by a long belt from the Machinery Floor, and it is the only machinery still working today higher than the first floor. By this time, there wasn't enough business to provide an income for a full-time miller, so Ben Davis worked at Hams Hall Power Station, and milled part-time. He converted New Hall Mill from being a flour mill into a grist mill, making animal feed from corn for local farmers instead. Ben also restored the Mill's vegetable garden, making it hugely productive. He grew a wide variety of fruit and vegetables, including cabbages, cauliflowers, beans, peas and carrots. Visitors to the Mill remember being given new potatoes from this wonderful garden. He also kept chickens, who laid lots of eggs.

In the 1960's, the Mill fell victim of to the march of modernisation. Because of flooding at the east end of New Hall Valley, Sutton Coldfield Council decided to restructure the course of the Plantsbrook, which had fed the Mill for centuries. The council put in a concrete bed to raise the level of the stream, but this starved the Mill of water. After hundreds of years of running on water, the Mill was now finally totally reliant on diesel.

Restoration of the Water Wheel

Sir Alfred Owen, however – despite suffering a stroke in 1969 - remained determined to see the water mill restored to working order. Owen's son, David Owen, supported him. In 1971, David Owen commissioned a survey to be carried out by local Sutton Coldfield surveyors, Bottley and Chaffer. By 1972, Derek Ogden, a millwright, and builders William Sapcote and Sons, started on the restoration project. This involved nurturing the ancient underground springs which still flowed into the mill stream. These springs were part of the same network that fed the New Hall Moat; they provided a consistent supply of water

that could be harnessed to power the water wheel.

The mill pond was dredged, and its retaining walls rebuilt, so that it was able to hold enough water to power the wheel. The leat - the stream that fed the mill pond - was cleared out, all the way to the New Hall Trout Pond upstream. Because the majority of water which had previously fed the mill pond, via the leat, no longer flowed from the Plantsbrook, a holding tank was installed with a recycling pump. This meant that water coming from the underground springs – which were powering the mill wheel - was recycled back to the pond, allowing for a steady stream of water. Many of the buckets on the water wheel itself also needed replacing. Because the bottom half of the wooden wheel had often sat in water when it was not being used, it had become heavily water-logged, which had unbalanced the wheel. The wooden buckets were replaced with iron, to ensure their longevity. The wooden pentrough – a sort of wooden tank - that fed the wheel with water from above, was rebuilt. Water once again became the driving force of New Hall Mill.

The buildings needed considerable restoration. Roof tiles and struts needed replacing. The wooden floors of the Mill had to be repaired and new staircases fitted, which would allow visitors to see the workings of the Mill. A fire escape system needed to be included, or the Mill wouldn't be able to open to the public. The original old staircase was preserved; with its narrow and worn wooden steps, it acts as a living testament to the generations of millers who have worked the Mill.

The extensive renovation project allowed Ben Davis to continue to process animal feed at the Mill, but he preferred to use the diesel engine to the newly-restored water wheel, as he found it more efficient. He occasionally put the water wheel to work grinding flour, to show visitors how it worked but, by the time he died in 1993, the water wheel was in need of repair again.

In 1975, so that the Mill could be preserved for the enjoyment and education of future generations, the Owen family established the New Hall Water Mill Preservation Trust. The Trust rented the Mill from Rubery Owen Holdings, to make the Mill accessible to visitors, and allow the trust to apply for grants for help with renovation and maintenance.

LEFT: Today, much care and attention has been paid to maintaining the dusty, noisy atmosphere of a working grain mill.

FOLLOWING PAGES: New Hall Mill as it is in 2022, restored to peak performance and with a brimming millpond once more.

LEFT: The loaves baked with flour ground at New Hall Mill in 1977, in celebration of the Queen's Silver Jubilee. Plans to bake bread for the Platinum Jubilee in 2022 were unfortunately cancelled due to the pandemic.

ABOVE: The original loaves baked for Queen Victoria in 1897 were found to have been preserved at the Windsor Castle Museum.

1977

Fit for a Queen and the Silver Jubilee

In 1977, when Queen Elizabeth celebrated her coronation's Silver Jubilee, the Mill ground some flour. The bakers G Golby of nearby Mere Green, Sutton Coldfield, then baked several loaves, as had been done for Queen Victoria in 1898. The loaves were delivered to Windsor, and some were used for a garden party that day. It was discovered, at this time, that some of the loaves baked for Queen Victoria in 1897, had been preserved in the Windsor Castle Museum. The thank you letter received from Buckingham Palace read:

"Thank you for very much for your letter of 3rd May which I was able to show to the Queen this morning, together with the brochure illustrating the New Hall Mill Restoration. Her Majesty will be delighted to accept some loaves of bread made from wheat grown on the farm and baked in the traditional manner at a local Sutton Coldfield Bakery. Her Majesty is most grateful to you for this interesting offer. I hope it will be possible for you to arrange to have roll baked, about six inches long. The reason I ask you to do this is that the Queen has a roll of about that length which was baked for Queen Victoria's Golden Jubilee. It would be interesting to preserve your roll and to see how it looks in fifty or sixty years' time!"

1990's

Following the death of Ben Davis, the tenancy of the Mill lay vacant for the first time in seventy years. Sir Alfred Owen had always hadthe vision after water was no longer available from Plants Brook to restore the Mill to full working order. As owners of the Mill it was the family company, Rubery Owen, that undertook to fulfil his wish. A survey of the Mill was organised, and the help of the Midlands Wind and Water Mills Group was enlisted – they had been frequent visitors to the Mill over the years when Ben Davis had been miller. At about the same time, members of the local history group of Sutton Coldfield, led by Roger Lea, established the Friends of New Hall Mill Group: this group's aims were to support both the renovations and the work of the Preservation Trust, in order to open the Mill regularly to the public. By 1996, the fully-restored Mill was opened to the public by the Lord Mayor of Birmingham, Councillor David Roy.

2001

In 2001, an extensive renovation project was started on the Mill's former stables to create a meeting room and toilets for visitors. As part of the renovations, the old stables were cleared out and corner joints were put in to hold up weak walls. A new drainage system had to be installed at one end to provide plumbing for the new toilets. The meeting room was underpinned and kitchen units installed. Inside walls were constructed out of brick to form visitor washroom facilities.A new tiled floor was installed in the stable. Brick work was repointed. Because the building was listed, no drainpipes were allowed to put on the outside of the old stables, so a pipe and gravel drainage system had to be installed around its base.

2021

Today, New Hall Mill is an oasis. It provides thousands of visitors a year with a unique insight into the workings of an original water mill. All the machinery has been carefully restored. On Open Days, it is operated by the Friends of New Hall Mill, to produce stone ground wholemeal flour. Much care and attention has been paid to maintaining the dusty, noisy atmosphere of a working grain mill. The cart shed that sits alongside the Mill houses additional machinery, as well as a farm-wagon. Near the entrance to the Mill, is the well from where millers drew their drinking water for hundreds of years. Thanks to the extensive renovations of the former stable and cowsheds, there is now an exhibition area, shop and tea-room and washrooms.

NO FISHING

LEFT: The overflow panel in 1952, with no overflow as the fragile system of springs that fed it were increasingly threatened by urban development, grew rusty and overgrown.

BELOW: Today, with new swales cut into the Plantsbrook river banks, and with a new sluice to control the level of water running into the mill pond, water levels are fully maintained and no longer dry up.

ABOVE: Ben Davis, grandson of Benjamin Styles, who was miller at New Shipton in 1901, continued as part-time miller until his retirement in 1980. He is seen here next to the large vegetable garden at the Mill, which would have provided the family with a steady supply of fresh produce.

FOLOWING PAGES: Luckily the vegetable garden has been restored to full magnificence, including a cereal cage growing the various types of wheat that can be ground for flour, a herb garden, cottage flower garden and tree trail. Plants are sold from the garden hut, and afternoon tea served on open days. What a transformation.

However, in the 1980's, the fragile system of springs feeding the Mill, which had been so carefully created back in the '70's, came under threat when a new housing development was built in Walmley, at the top of the valley. Land in New Hall Valley was also handed over to the council to build a Country Park. As all the old springs feeding the millstream were doomed to be severed by the development work, new swales were cut to ensure water would still flow down to the old mill stream. A new sluice was put in, to control the level of the water running to the mill pool. This system appears to continue to maintain the water levels effectively to this day.

The garden that surrounds the Mill House still includes the large vegetable garden that would have provided the miller and his family with a steady supply of fresh produce. This garden is now looked after by the Friends.

A short path passing through the trees next to the cart shed offers fine views of the mill pond. The pond itself is home to wild ducks, herons and kingfishers. A longer path runs through the mill meadow, where there are two smaller ponds and native trees. The Mill is an escape from the outside world, a way to get back to nature – as well as back in time.

Ghosts of New Hall Mill

It has long been accepted that New Hall Mill houses the ghosts of previous millers and their families. Ben Davis used to tell visitors that, when he was a child, he and his father would often hear a sharp knocking at the door - but when they went to open it, nobody was there.

One day, at their front door, appeared an elderly man, who had lived at the Mill before Benjamin Styles, Ben Davis's grandfather. The man recounted how he had often had strange experiences while living there. He specifically asked Ben's mother if she had every noticed the iron stove doors opening and closing of their own accord, which she confirmed. Previous occupants of the Mill have told similar stories.

Acknowledgements

Several years ago, my godfather, David Owen, who had always been a staunch supporter of my career as a photojournalist, came to view an exhibition I was included in at the Midland Arts Centre (MAC). He asked if I might know anyone who could help him produce a book about New Hall, using the many photographs and documents he had collected over the years.

I had visited New Hall as a child and it was a place that had always intrigued me. Having studied Medieval history at university, the story of the house fascinated me. David also showed me photographs taken of his father, Alfred Owen, at New Hall by Henri Cartier Bresson, a photographer whose work I had always admired. These compelling factors inspired me to spend the last three years bringing the contents of this book together.

I could not have achieved this without the many people who have helped me along the way: David and Ethne Owen for their hospitality while researching the book, and for handing over reams of information and family material about New Hall. David in particular for his enthusiasm for New Hall, its history and his family who have had such a huge influence on not only Sutton Coldfield's development over the years but also more widely on the UK motor industry.

Nadene Ghouri for her edits, and Charlotte Eagar for taking my very long history essay and turning into something so much more!

Ruth Wagget for her diligence in organising a lot of the material.

Friends of New Hall Mill, Marian Baxter, the Birmingham Library and the Sutton Coldfield History Society for a huge amount of the information found in the book.

James Wiseman – the General Manager of New Hall and Thistle Hotels, for allowing us to stay to take up to date photographs of the house and garden, and his enthusiasm for the project.

Jim Owen for his stories of growing up at New Hall

Andrew my husband for his patience with piles of photos cluttering up our dining room table.

And finally to my father for introducing me to David, making him my godfather, and for taking me to New Hall in 1976 – the early trip which inspired this book.

Kate Holt
Chute Lodge
August 2022

Bibliography

Charters, Records and Grants of Arms – The Royal Town of Sutton Coldfield published 1935 by the Borough Council

Ghost Stories of Sutton Coldfield by Patrick B. Hayes, published 2000 Brewin Books

Glimpse into Sutton's Past Part 2 1851 – 1885 by Stephen Roberts, published 2021 APS Books, Stourbridge

History of The Forest and Chase of Sutton Coldfield, published 1867 Simpkin, Marshall & Co,London

Memorials of Old Warwickshire edited by Alice Dryden, published 1908 Bemrose and Sons Ltd

Memories of Rubery Owen compiled by R J Owen, 2005 Rubery Owen Holdings Ltd

New Hall – The First 800 Years – Marvyn, Sutton Coldfield Library 1988

New Shipton Farm – Archaeological Evaluation published 1995 by the Oxford Archaeological Unit

Sutton Coldfield – A Pictorial History by Sue Bates, published 1997 Phillimore

Sutton Coldfield Towns and Chase by W Midgley, published 1904 in The Midland Counties Herald

Tales of a Bishop..and a Royal Town by J E Willmott, published 1948 by Green and Welburn Ltd

The Bishop Vesey Houses and other Old buildings in Sutton Coldfield by P. B. Chatwin and E. G. Harcourt, reprinted from the Birmingham Archaeological Society and Transactions and Proceedings for the years 1941 and 1942 by Charles Batey, University Press Oxford

The New Hall Estate – Notes by A F Fentiman, published 1996 by The Sutton Coldfield Local History Research Group

The Trial of Doctor Henry Sacheverell published 1710 by the House of Peers

The Trial of Doctor Sacheverell by Geoffrey Holmes, published 1973 Eyre Methuen Ltd

Wincelle by A F Fentiman, published 1998 by The Sutton Coldfield Local History Research Group

INDEX

T

V

W

Y